DATE DUE

UNDERSTANDING
LITERATURE

A Student's Guide to

JOHN
STEINBECK

Gerald Newman and
Eleanor Newman Layfield

Enslow Publishers, Inc.

40 Industrial Road	PO Box 38
Box 398	Aldershot
Berkeley Heights, NJ 07922	Hants GU12 6BP
USA	UK

http://www.enslow.com

For Juliane Quinn Newman

The authors gratefully acknowledge the immeasurable assistance of Julia Kots in the preparation of this book.

Library of Congress Cataloging-in-Publication Data

Newman, Gerald.
    A student's guide to John Steinbeck / Gerald Newman, Eleanor Newman Layfield.
        p. cm.
    Includes bibliographical references and index.
    ISBN 0-7660-2259-5
    1. Steinbeck, John, 1902-1968. 2. Novelists, American--20th century-- Biography. I. Title.
    PS3537.T3234Z777   2004
    813'.52--dc22

                                            2004002304

Printed in the United States of America

10 9 8 7 6 5 4 3 2 1

To Our Readers:
We have done our best to make sure all Internet addresses in this book were active and appropriate when we went to press. However, the author and the publisher have no control over and assume no liability for the material available on those Internet sites or on other Web sites they may link to. Any comments or suggestions can be sent by e-mail to comments@enslow.com or to the address on the back cover.

Illustration Credits: AP/Wide World Photos, p. 12; ArtToday.com, p. 135; Library of Congress, pp. 59, 68; courtesy of the Cold Spring Harbor Laboratory, p. 147.

Cover Illustration: AP/Wide World Photos (inset); Corel Corporation/ Hemera Technologies, Inc./ Library of Congress (background objects).

CONTENTS

1 Roots of a Writer........................ 5

2 Published Success..................... 20

3 *Of Mice and Men* 35

4 Writing the First "Big Book" 48

5 *The Grapes of Wrath* 64

6 Coping with Fame 88

7 The Last Big Book.................... 102

8 *East of Eden* 108

9 A Writer Writes as He Lives.......... 124

10 The Measure of This Man 144

Chronology........................ 159

Chapter Notes....................... 162

Glossary 169

Selected Published Works
of John Steinbeck 170

Further Reading
and Internet Addresses 173

Index 174

CHAPTER 1

ROOTS OF A WRITER

The Salinas Valley is . . . a long narrow swale between two ranges of mountains, and the Salinas River winds and twists up the center until it falls at last into Monterey Bay. . . .

From both sides of the valley little streams slipped out of the hill canyons and fell into the bed of the Salinas River. In the winter of wet years the streams ran full-freshet, and they swelled the river until sometimes it raged and boiled. . . . Then when late spring came the river drew in from its edges and the sand bank appeared. . . . The Salinas was only a part time river. The summer drove it underground. . . .

But there were dry years too, and they put terror on the valley. . . . And it never failed that during the dry years the people forgot about the rich years, and during the wet years they lost all memory of the dry years. It was always that way.

And this is about the way the Salinas Valley was when my grandfather brought his wife and settled in the foothills.[1]

This is how John Ernst Steinbeck III begins *East of*

Eden, his best-selling novel, published in 1952. He sets it in Salinas, a town with a population of about 2,500, fifteen miles east of Monterey Bay. Many of Steinbeck's novels and short stories take place in or around the California town. Many of his essays recall his youth there. Salinas was his family's home, the place where he was born on February 27, 1902.

John's mother, Olive, was an active member of Salinas society. She was a fund-raiser who planned community functions for the town. Through Olive's connections, John's father, John Ernst Steinbeck II, was able to become town treasurer, a position he held until his death in 1936. Though the Steinbecks were never really wealthy (at one point John Ernst II went bankrupt), they were financially secure. The Steinbecks were the typical churchgoing family, with three daughters, Beth (1894–1992), Esther (1892–1986), Mary (1905–1965), and one son, John.

YOUNG JOHN

For his first few years, John's face showed signs of his difficult birth. His mother called him "little squirrel" and his sisters referred to him as "muskrat." The nicknames were meant affectionately, but they were disturbing to John who was very sensitive about his looks. Most people believed he was not very good-looking.[2] His ears stuck out and he was plagued by acne well into his college years. Because John was the only boy, his sisters fussed over him and his father expected more from him than he did from his daughters. John took full advantage of his position in the household by often getting into trouble. Mary and older sister Beth took good care of him, but both considered him "spoiled."[3]

In 1908, the Steinbecks enrolled John in the Baby School, the primary school on Central Avenue. He was far ahead of his classmates in reading because of tutoring from his mother, Olive, a chore John never liked.[4] John was a loner, spending much of his free time playing in his backyard or reading in his room. He enjoyed books such as *Alice in Wonderland* and *Tom Brown's Schooldays*, but myths and legends were his favorites, especially Sir Thomas Malory's *Morte D'Arthur*.[5] John's younger sister, Mary, remained John's confidante through most of his adolescence. She took on the role of best friend when he had no friends and shared with him a unique rapport.[6]

HIGH SCHOOL

When he entered Salinas High School in 1915, John Steinbeck remained mostly out of touch with his peers. He never volunteered in class and worked just hard enough to get slightly above-average grades. John hardly dated nor was he invited to parties, and he was rarely part of group activities or events. However, he did get along with a few boys on a one-to-one basis. One was Max Wagner, who lived in Mexico before coming to Salinas. Together they befriended some of the town's Mexican teenagers.

Though his high school yearbook indicates that he was a member of the track, football, and basketball teams, his awkward size and ungainliness attributed to his failure as an athlete. He was also a failure as a member of the student training corps, a volunteer group like Junior R.O.T.C. that aided in the war effort. He hated marching around in a uniform, and he hated even more getting up before dawn. However, with a total school population of one hundred students, everyone was expected to participate in activities. In addition to athletics and the training corps, John also joined the drama society and the science club. He was elected senior class president and associate editor of the yearbook, a position he enjoyed and at which he was successful.[7] A student a year younger than John remarked: "John was known as a writer even then. He would get you in a corner and spin a hell of a yarn. From what people said to me at the time, he wrote a good bit of the yearbook all by himself. It just didn't surprise any of us when he became famous for his books."[8]

In June 1919, just after World War I ended, John graduated from Salinas High School. He was off to Stanford University, happy for a chance to get out of Salinas.

A LAZY STUDENT

John agreed to go to college only if he could study writing, much to his parents' dismay. John was enrolled at Stanford, off and on, from the fall of 1919 to the spring of 1925. He was an English major, concentrating on creative writing. He studied Greek and Latin and participated in the army's ROTC, riding the corps' horses when they were not used for training.

Unfortunately, he also brought his lackadaisical attitude to college. Even worse, he became a poker player and a drinker. Late nights of card games, drinking, and carousing meant missed classes and late assignments. Probation notices constantly followed him. John rarely completed courses, often dropping them in mid-semester. All told, he earned only three years of credit in the six years he was at Stanford. Without George Mors, Steinbeck's roommate, a straitlaced, clean-cut young man who tried to look after him, Steinbeck might not have gotten that far.

The summer after his first year at college, John got a job working in a factory along with Mors. By summer's end, Steinbeck decided he would put off returning to school and continue working instead. He would not return to Stanford until the fall of 1921.

SECOND YEAR

When Steinbeck returned to Stanford, he remained on probation. Many of the problems he had before remained unresolved, such as his tendency to spend more time in the library reading material of his own choosing rather than what his professors required.

That Christmas, Steinbeck went to Oakland and stayed with a friend, Robert Bennett. He found a temporary job at Capwell's Department Store, selling men's clothes. Then he got a job as part of a dredging crew to dig a ditch from Salinas to Castroville so that markers could be placed to indicate a canal route. He hated to be doing manual labor again, but he was well-liked by the men he worked with. They taught "Johnny boy," as they called him, to gamble, to drink, and to smoke marijuana.

On one occasion, Steinbeck offered a group of men money for any stories they could tell him about themselves. A young man named Frank Kilkenny told him about a kind farmwife who nursed him with her breastmilk when he was on the brink of starvation. Steinbeck was so moved by the story that he gave Kilkenny two dollars, a large sum of money in 1922.

Steinbeck then worked at a ranch, as a foreman of Mexican and Filipino workers who hauled heavy bags of beets onto trucks. In the evenings he would sit with his men and listen to them talk about their lives. He knew that to be successful at this job, the men—tough, illiterate vagabonds—had to respect him, so he worked much harder than they did. After four months he quit and returned to his parents' home. He read all day and drank all night with no clue as to why his writing was not what he wanted it to be. At his father's insistence, he even sought psychological help from a family doctor who thought John's problem was caused by a low-grade viral infection. Then one night, as he scrawled on his pad, he realized that he had accumulated all these notes about the people he had met: the downtrodden, penniless underclass he so respected and admired.

Writing at School

Steinbeck returned to Stanford in the winter of 1923, believing that this time he was more mature, more determined to actually become a writer, more aware of who he really was. This time his grades were A's and B's. At registration he ran into a classmate, Carlton Sheffield, known as "Dook," whom he had met in French class when they were freshmen. Because the two found common ground in being English majors, hoping to become professional writers, and both having a strange sense of humor, they quickly became roommates and close friends.

Steinbeck was well aware of class and race distinctions on campus and did what he could to thumb his nose at those distinctions. One time he brought a Chinese date to the prom, which shocked both the students and the faculty. On another occasion he decided to challenge the policy of not allowing drinking on campus. He sat down in front of a palm tree near the Memorial Church on the Inner Quad, a gallon of red wine in tow, and spent the night drinking. In addition, he had altered the carillon in the church to play "How Dry I Am," a drinking song. The dean was not amused.

Steinbeck became a driving force in the English Club, not only because he was constantly writing and needed a forum to present his work, but also because it earned him acknowledgment by members of the faculty.

Edith Ronald Mirrielees, a short-story writing teacher, was Steinbeck's greatest influence at Stanford. She forced him to say what he meant rather than allow him to

11

JOHN STEINBECK

Renowned novelist and writer, John Steinbeck.

overwrite. She forced him to make revisions, which he often resisted. She made him write clearly, simply, and succinctly. In short, she helped to turn him into a professional. He became her top student of all time. She rewarded him with a grade of B, which annoyed Steinbeck, but he understood it was given so that he would continue to work harder.[9] Years later she occasionally spoke about Steinbeck in her class. Her only negative comment was that he was too sentimental even in his later works. She said she wished he had eliminated the last few paragraphs of *Of Mice and Men*.[10]

During the summer of 1924, Steinbeck again returned to Salinas and was joined by his friend Dook Sheffield. After working for a few months on the night shift at the factory, Steinbeck took a final turn at Stanford. This time, however, he avoided the dorm, and instead, rented a toolshed attached to a barn behind a house on Palo Alto Avenue. It had no electricity, no gas, and no water. He cleared a living area about six feet square where he placed an army cot, a wooden box which held an old Corona typewriter, and an assemblage of gallon jugs for the wine he planned to make. He paid five dollars to rent the home he called "The Sphincter." The room was alternately dubbed "The Den of Pegasus." Invoking the image of the mythical flying horse was meant to represent the fantastical dreams of John and his fellow writers. He later decided that it should not be a flying horse, but a flying pig, which he dubbed "Pigagus": "a lumbering soul but trying to fly," with "not enough wingspread but plenty of intention."[11]

One reason Steinbeck chose to live in seclusion was so he could concentrate on writing without being disturbed by outside influences. He also began making wine at home. John befriended fellow English Club member Elizabeth Smith, who went by the pen name John Breck. The two threw many parties at her house. Dook Sheffield realized the importance of John's relationship with Breck: "This is John's real university. Everything was up for *discussion*: music, books, politics. I think everyone was surprised by how knowledgeable John was. It would have surprised most of his professors."[12]

Steinbeck's writing was going well. He had completed several stories, some of which even he thought were good. He showed one of them, "A Lady in Infra-Red," to Breck who immediately recognized it as autobiographical. Breck saw the faults in the story but convinced John to expand it into a full-length novel. Steinbeck expanded the story into an allegory about a poor Welsh boy who runs off to the Caribbean to find his fortune. But when he has no luck and becomes a pirate, he is forever banished from returning home. By May he had completed forty pages, which Breck's daughter Polly typed for him. But because he spent so much time working on the novel, Stanford again warned him that he was facing suspension since he had missed so many classes.

ALLEGORY—*A symbolic representation or expression.*

14

NEW YORK

Steinbeck left Stanford for good in 1925. His father even offered to give him an allowance of twenty dollars a month for six months so that he could complete the novel. Steinbeck went off to the cottage in Pacific Grove to meet the deadline, but the more he wrote the more he hated the book. In October 1925, he took the manuscript to John Breck who refused to read it because she was angry over his leaving school. He then brought the novel to Edith Mirrielees who, after reading it, told him to forget it and return to Stanford for more education and experience. Steinbeck told his father he was not returning to school and he would no longer ask him for support.[13]

Steinbeck decided to go to New York to become a reporter. He eventually settled in his sister Beth's walk-up apartment in the Fort Greene section of Brooklyn. He found a job at a construction company that was building the new Madison Square Garden on Eighth Avenue and Fiftieth Street in Manhattan. After fifteen to eighteen hours a day of hauling wheelbarrows filled with cement up ramps to men high up in the scaffolding, he was exhausted by the time he got back to Brooklyn each night. His sister remembers him eating a sandwich for dinner and then going directly to bed without ever writing a word. It was a job he could not keep. Finally, after seeing a coworker fall from the scaffolding to his death, Steinbeck quit.

Steinbeck's maternal uncle, Joe Hamilton, got him a position on William Randolph Hearst's *New York American* as a cub reporter. He combed the streets for stories and usually found them, but his reportage suffered from the same problems as his work in college: it was too flowery, too overwritten. He was reassigned to the courts down in the Park Row section of Manhattan where the hardened reporters there could train him. He remembers playing bridge, sharing the liquor given to the reporters by judges who confiscated it because of Prohibition, and becoming a much better reporter. He found it "a happy place to work."[14] With the little money he was now earning, Steinbeck moved into the Parkwood Hotel near Gramercy Park in Manhattan. He lived in a dingy, bug-infested apartment on the sixth floor. His rent was seven dollars a week. Along with Ted Miller, a friend from Stanford who had also moved to New York, Steinbeck spent nights sampling local restaurants and discovering the city. Sometimes he covered a trial; sometimes he ventured into Brooklyn or Queens to cover a story; more often he got lost in Brooklyn or Queens. Eventually, he got fired.

Steinbeck sent some of his stories to Guy Holt, a friend who worked for Robert M. McBride and Company, a small publishing house that took an interest in new writers. Holt liked what he read and promised Steinbeck he would publish a collection of his work if Steinbeck would submit six more stories as good as the first ones. During the next few weeks, Steinbeck worked feverishly to finish the stories. When they were done, Holt was no longer with the company and the new editor had no interest in publishing the collection of stories. Steinbeck was so enraged that he began shouting and cursing and physically assaulting the editor.[15] Holt's new employer, the John Day Company, was equally uninterested in the short stories. Holt suggested that John go home and write a novel.[16]

Writer's Block

Steinbeck returned home as a steward on a ship going back to San Francisco. He served food, cleaned up, and in his spare time wrote letters for the crewmembers and even beat up the ship's bully. Then he joined Toby Street at Lake Tahoe for the rest of the summer. Ultimately, Steinbeck spent more time writing to friends to tell them about his loneliness and writer's block than he did writing the novel. In March 1927, with no luck on the novel, he tackled an old short story, "The Gifts of Iban," he had started at Stanford. Once it was rewritten, he sent it off under the pen name John Stern to an obscure magazine called *The Smoker's Companion*. The magazine published it, paid him a royalty of seven dollars, and asked for more stories. He never told his family or friends he had made the sale.[17]

A Special Stenographer

By the end of January 1928, Steinbeck's novel was done. The short story "A Lady in Infra-Red" was transformed into the novel *The Pot of Gold*, and then retitled *Cup of Gold*.

But Steinbeck hated it. He mailed it to Ted Miller, but Miller returned the manuscript because it was handwritten. Steinbeck needed a stenographer—someone to type up what he had written. He eventually found one, a woman, named Carol Henning. She was twenty-two years old and was vacationing from San Francisco with her sister Idell at Lake Tahoe. At first Steinbeck did not think Henning was very pretty, but he admired her personality and forthright attitude.[18] He offered her a nickel a page to type the work and within days she presented him with a neatly composed manuscript. Henning thought very highly of the novel and could not understand Steinbeck's fears about it. She so enjoyed being part of the manuscript-to-printed-page process that she refused to take any money for her work. Steinbeck was distraught when she and her sister left. He knew he had to see Carol Henning again.

Soon after, Steinbeck left for San Francisco. His sister Mary's new husband, Bill Decker, whose family owned part of the Bemis Bag company, got him a job in a warehouse hauling heavy bales of jute or hemp on hand trucks. Whenever Steinbeck was not hauling bales of sacks into storage or attempting unsuccessfully to write, he was running around town with Henning, having inexpensive dinners in North Beach or hopping the streetcars to spend a day at the beach.

In October, Steinbeck moved into the top floor of a walk-up on Powell Street. It had the traditional Steinbeck look, complete with mice "scratching all night in the walls and ceilings." As his sister Mary recalled: "He never minded being down-and-out. I think he actually liked it. Young writers were supposed to be poor."[19] The San Francisco experience was a pleasant one, even though it was not financially rewarding. Steinbeck would read chapters to the Henning sisters and when he was not working, would drop in at local discussion groups whose members discussed current happenings, probably including the effects of the Depression on workers. Steinbeck used the few dollars he had left to buy Carol Henning's old Buick and returned to Pacific Grove. At least there he could live rent-free and concentrate on writing without having to worry about where the next dollar came from. His father, optimistic that *Cup of Gold* would earn some money, again offered him an allowance until royalties began coming in.

PUBLISHED
SUCCESS

Cup of Gold was finished in the fall of 1929, but Steinbeck was truly embarrassed by it. Though he refused to admit it, his new influence was Ernest Hemingway. Undoubtedly, Carol Henning was a strong factor in John's newfound enthusiasm for writing and had suggested he read Hemingway. She believed in Steinbeck perhaps more than he believed in himself. She observed and coached and edited and did everything else she could to help him become the writer he wanted to be.

At last Cup of Gold found a publisher. In early 1930, Robert M. McBride and Company consented to release the book. Even though this was the same publisher that rejected his stories a few years before, Steinbeck decided to go with McBride because it was more enthusiastic than any other publishing company about the possible success of the book. They even contracted Steinbeck's friend Mahlon Blaine to design the dust cover.

When summer arrived, Steinbeck moved to Palo Alto to live with Dook Sheffield and his second wife, Maryon. Dook had returned to Stanford to work on his master's degree. On weekends he and Dook would edit what Steinbeck had written during the week and Henning, who would take the train down from San Francisco, would type the revised pages. In August, Henning used her vacation time to go camping with Steinbeck in the hills of La Honda, near Palo Alto. Each morning Steinbeck would wander off into the woods to a tree stump he used as a desk. He would set out his pens and bottle of ink and devote himself entirely to neatly entering his novel into a ledger.

Cup of Gold was finally published in August 1930. Steinbeck earned a small royalty, enough for him to live comfortably for a short while.

LIVING WITH CAROL HENNING

John Steinbeck and Carol Henning were similar in many ways: they were both bright, stubborn, and independent. They knew how to have fun, laugh at life's absurdities, and though they saw the dark side of almost everything, they could also stand back and dismiss it. Their differences were more important. Much like his father, Steinbeck was quiet, even withdrawn, but still argumentative, while Henning was assertive and funny. He was plagued by mood swings, while she was rock-solid. He was insecure about his prospects while she believed he had a profitable and fulfilling future.

Steinbeck and Henning decided to get married.

Together they moved in with Dook Sheffield and his wife in their house near Occidental College in Los Angeles and then rented a dump of a house in the same Eagle Rock neighborhood. The rent was a mere fifteen dollars a month.[1] On January 14, 1930, the Sheffields escorted John Steinbeck and Carol Henning to the courthouse in Glendale, where they were married, without ever having told his or her parents or friends about the event.[2] Through it all John Steinbeck continued to write and by the spring of 1930 *To the Unknown God* was finished. It was based on his maternal grandparents, the Hamiltons, but used the story of his grandfather Steinbeck's migration from New England to California.

It was a happy time for them all. The Steinbecks did not have much money, but John was productive and Carol seemed to be a good influence on his work. In June, they moved to a wood-frame house in Tujunga, not far from Eagle Rock. With the help of John's father, Carol Steinbeck found a job as the secretary to the Secretary of the Chamber of Commerce in Monterey. John Steinbeck, who felt both energized and at peace, began spending about five hours a day writing a new book.

To an Unknown God (the title was revised) could not find a publisher. No one seemed to be interested in a psychological novel about a paranoid individual, especially during the Depression. Steinbeck was disappointed but undaunted. He wrote to Carol: "I have high hopes for myself. . . . Eventually I shall be so good that I cannot be ignored. These years are disciplinary for me."[3]

MEETING RICKETTS

Steinbeck met Edward F. Ricketts at the dentist's. Ricketts was extremely bright, well-educated (but with no degrees), and, like Steinbeck, a loner, an individual, an iconoclast, and prone to drinking too much. Ricketts was the owner of Pacific Biological Laboratories, Inc., situated in an old house on Cannery Row in Monterey. The rooms in the house were all converted to museum-like showrooms, some displaying marine specimens, rattlesnakes, and white rats. Another room was set up with slide preparation material and microscopes for viewing slides of the organisms Ricketts brought in from the sea. It was an array of cluttered, messy rooms filled with whatever live or preserved specimens Ricketts could provide for high school and college biology labs and government research facilities.

Steinbeck did not make friends easily but Ricketts was that rare combination of scientist, philosopher, nonconformist, poet, and intellectual that Steinbeck was, or at least wished he could be. So strong was their bond that traits of Ed Ricketts appear in characters in several of Steinbeck's works.

Ricketts tried to explain to Steinbeck that he need not write obscure allegories and that his characters need not be symbols of great worldly concepts. For example, they could be about all the people on Cannery Row, where they were drinking beer at that moment: the fisherman, the

SYMBOL—*Something that stands for, represents, or suggests another thing.*

cannery workers, the barflies, and the prostitutes. Ricketts wanted Steinbeck to be a "scientist of the imagination."[4] He also wanted Steinbeck to observe people he met and, like a scientist, classify them so he could use the data when necessary.

By the spring of 1931, Carol lost her job and the Steinbecks were feeling the strains of poverty more than ever. The old Chevy was hardly in any condition to be used even if there had been money for gas. Steinbeck's only diversion was his daily walk down to Ricketts' lab and Sunday visits with his parents.

SYMBOLISM— *The representation of things by use of symbols.*

John remembered Carol's friend Beth telling them about a little valley, Corral de Tierra, where her aunt lived and how it would make a great locale for a book about the odd people who lived there. Whether or not he used her idea has never been proved, but soon he wrote to Ted Miller to describe *The Pastures of Heaven* as a series of related short stories centered around the Munroe family who live in a small valley and interacted with an array of local folks, each of whom come to a sorry end.

On February 27, 1932, John's thirtieth birthday, he received a telegram from McIntosh and Otis that the publishers Cape and Smith had accepted his manuscript of *The Pastures of Heaven.* He was more concerned about his parents' reaction than his own. "I'm no longer a white elephant. I am justified in the eyes of their neighbors," was his comment.[5]

It was now time for Steinbeck to concentrate on a

total rewrite of *To an Unknown God*, to turn it into a better constructed work. He was preparing it for Robert O. Ballou, his new editor at McIntosh and Otis, who was extremely impressed with *Pastures of Heaven*. Moreover, now he could write while breathing a bit easier. Ricketts had hired Carol as his part-time secretary/assistant for $50 a month. But then, life went sour. John's young nephew, his sister Beth's son, died; John's publisher went bankrupt; John's editor joined a new publishing firm; Ricketts' wife left him; Ricketts fired Carol; and Joseph Campbell moved into the community.

Campbell was a young Columbia University-educated author who admired Steinbeck's writing and recognized his talent. Unfortunately, he also was in love with Carol. After a brief affair, he admitted everything to Steinbeck and moved to New York.[6]

The Pastures of Heaven did not do well with the public. One reason may have been that it was 1933: the Depression had worsened and unemployment rose to 12 million people. People who could hardly buy bread were clearly not buying books. Steinbeck suggested to Mavis McIntosh that she separate his book, which was really a murder mystery, into chapters and offer them to a pulp magazine for serialization.

OLIVE'S LAST DAYS

The Steinbecks had no money coming in except for the monthly stipend from his father, John Ernst, and because of the economy there was no guarantee how long that was going to last. When John Ernst and Olive invited John and Carol home for the holidays, they had to foot the bill for the couple's trip. When the young couple arrived in Salinas, they discovered that Olive was failing fast and though she insisted on cooking, Carol needed to stand behind her to prevent her from falling over. Both the Steinbeck men were filled with dread—John Ernst because of his constant dependence on Olive's endurance and John because he was afraid his mother would die knowing him only as a failure. The pervading gloom was nearly unbearable.

In March, Olive suffered a stroke. John and Carol moved into the house in Salinas to help care for her. John spent the better part of the day at the hospital hating every minute of seeing the strong woman he remembered deteriorating so rapidly.

At that time John sporadically worked on a short story about a boy whose pony develops a fatal disease, distemper. He heard from Robert Ballou, who was determined to publish *To an Unknown God* himself. He would act as agent, editor and publisher, but his option, or right to publish, on the book had run out before he had the financial backing. In the meantime, McIntire and Otis had gotten Simon and Schuster, a very prestigious publisher, to commit. However, broke or not, Steinbeck remembered how loyal Ballou had been to him and agreed to extend his option to publish the book though the contract had run out.

PHALANX THEORY

One day in June, as John sat by his mother's bedside, an odd thought crossed his mind. "Half of the cell units in my mother's body have rebelled. . . . She, as a human unit, is deterred from functioning as she ordinarily did by a schism of a number of her cells."[7]

He remembered how this idea fit in with the ideas of William Emerson Ritter. Under Ricketts' supervision, Steinbeck eventually wrote a paper (though it was never published) called "Argument of Phalanx." In essence, Steinbeck's premise was that when you are part of a group there is no "you." You behave as the group behaves. Once a person is removed from the group, the person becomes a phalanx, a unit made of cells. Steinbeck based the thesis on Ritter's claim that each of the pieces of the whole is equally

PHALANX—*An organized group of people.*

important to the whole's ability to function. Like all units made up of parts, Steinbeck conjectured, people in groups connect through a stronger spirit that moves them from within. In his own words: "Man is a unit of the greater beasts, the phalanx. The phalanx has pains, desires, hungers, and strivings as different as those from the unit man's are different from the [body's] cells. . . . Within . . . his subconscious, there is a keying device with which he may become part of the phalanx." He concluded that a human is a "double thing—a group animal and at the same time an individual."[8] Think of a school of fish all swimming in one direction. They, as a group, are the

27

phalanx. But if one fish swims away, it is vulnerable and the phalanx will not protect it. Therefore it must be its own phalanx. That idea would pervade Steinbeck's work from then on.

Strangely enough, with less time to work, Steinbeck became more creative. He finished what he called the "pony book." He then went on to write the *paisano* stories based on his many encounters with the locals in Cannery Row and the stories told to him by Sue Gregory, a high school Spanish teacher of Mexican heritage who had been studying the local Mexicans living nearby in a shabby district known as Tortilla Flat. It was not a hard book for Steinbeck to write because he had had an affinity for Mexican-Americans since his childhood.

By October 1933, Robert Ballou kept his promise and published *To a God Unknown*. It is a mythical tale of a man named Joseph Wayne, who tries to fulfill his dead father's dream of creating a prosperous farm in California. In the process, he finds a tree on his property that embodies his father's spirit, but one of his brothers, afraid of paganism, chops it down. Thereafter, Joseph's farm suffers famine and pestilence. *To a God Unknown* received the same kind of limited reception as *The Pastures of Heaven*. But Ballou and McIntire and Otis still believed in Steinbeck even though as a professional author of seven years, he had earned only $870. Elizabeth Otis, however, was able to place two sections of *The Red Pony* into two consecutive issues of the prestigious monthly magazine, *North American Review*. The magazine paid Steinbeck $90. Carol found a job with the Emergency Relief Organization, a government agency that helped mostly Mexican families to find work. Her nightly tales of their horrific lives gave John more background for his *paisano* novel.

As a break from caring for his parents, John would take long walks. On one of them he noticed cars and trucks with Oklahoma license plates overflowing with furniture and people in tattered clothes. A small enclave had been set up that the Salinas people called "Little Oklahoma." Curious to learn about these displaced "Okies," Steinbeck sat down with some of them to chat about why and how they crossed the country to find work in California. He found them fascinating and told Carol that their story would make a great novel.

On February 19, 1934, as John sat by her bedside, Olive died peacefully in her sleep.

John finished his *paisano* book that he called *Tortilla Flat* and sent it first to Mavis McIntosh and then to Robert Ballou, who both rejected it. Steinbeck then decided to follow Ricketts' suggestion that he concentrate on writing more short stories.

COMMUNISM

Because he sympathized with the downtrodden and felt an affinity for some of the idealistic principles behind Communism, Steinbeck was often accused of being a Communist. But Steinbeck was never a member of the Communist Party. Among the many reasons for

Steinbeck's rejection of Communism was his strong belief in the individual and not in the "collective." Still, Steinbeck was interested in telling the story of Pat Chambers and Caroline Decker, two union organizers of the Cannery and Agricultural Workers' Industrial Union (C&AWIU) who were hiding out in Seaside, a small town near Monterey, to avoid being arrested for illegal strike activity. They were soon joined by Cicil McKiddy, who was instrumental in winning the cotton workers strike in Bakersfield the year before. McKiddy, originally from the dust bowl of Oklahoma, had been a publicist for the union in Monterey, writing and printing pamphlets about the plight of the workers, which was the reason the Monterey police were after him. Steinbeck offered to pay the three a small sum to write about them because he knew instinctively their story of labor activism was a good one.

Meanwhile, Pascal "Pat" Covici, a partner in a New York publishing company, Covici-Friede, read a copy of *The Pastures of Heaven* and immediately called McIntosh and Otis to ask if they had any unpublished Steinbeck manuscripts. They sent him *Tortilla Flat*. Covici loved the novel and offered not only to publish it, but to republish any Steinbeck novels that had gone out of print and to publish any subsequent novels Steinbeck would write.

By the end of January 1935, Steinbeck finished the 120,000-word manuscript of *In Dubious Battle* but Covici-Friede rejected it. At this point Elizabeth Otis took over Steinbeck's career. She thought highly of him as an author and admired him as a person. They were actually a perfect professional pair. Otis sent the new manuscript to Bobbs-Merrill, a large publishing house that agreed to publish it. Pat Covici was furious when he returned from vacation to discover that without authorization Harry Black, one of his editors, had rejected *In Dubious Battle*. Black took it upon himself to decline the book because he thought its story of workers' rights would offend some readers. Covici fired Black and pleaded with Steinbeck to get *In Dubious Battle* back from Bobbs-Merrill and allow Covici-Friede to publish it. Steinbeck agreed and a lifelong partnership began.

John Ernst died in May, five days before his son's new book, *Tortilla Flat*, appeared in bookstores. A retelling of the legend of King Arthur set in the slums of Monterey, an examination of the phalanx as seen in gang life, and a wry comment on possessions as economic status symbols, *Tortilla Flat* was well-received by most critics, but it was the reading public that made it a best-seller. Readers enjoyed Steinbeck's comical approach and the truthful portrayal of the harsh conditions of their lives. In mid-August, Pat Covici handed Steinbeck his first royalty check. It was for $300. John and Carol's days of abject poverty were over.

The film rights to *Tortilla Flat* eventually sold for $4,000. John and Carol went to New York in January 1936 to sign the contracts and then returned to Pacific Grove to enjoy their newfound wealth. They soon learned that *Tortilla Flat* had just hit the bestseller list and had been awarded the 1935 prize by the Commonwealth Club of

California, for being the best novel about California. It earned the distinction of being one of the five best-selling books on the West Coast.

IN DUBIOUS BATTLE

In Dubious Battle was published in January 1936 to generally good reviews, though not as good as those for *Tortilla Flat*. Some conservatives thought *In Dubious Battle* was a pro-Communist treatise because it depicted the exploitation of the lower classes by wealthy businessmen and landowners, while some liberals thought it completely distorted Communist ideology. The distinguished French author and future Nobel Prize recipient Andre Gide called *In Dubious Battle* "a beautiful and painful book."[9] Mary McCarthy, fresh out of Vassar, wrote a very negative review in the *Nation*. She commented that Steinbeck was "no philosopher, sociologist or strike tactician" and used terms like "childish" and "pompous" to describe his writing.[10] Steinbeck was more annoyed than he was pleased that his book was selling well. The critics, even those who reviewed the novel favorably, had misunderstood his message.

In Dubious Battle tells the story of a workers' strike in California apple country. The leader, Jim Nolan, an idealist devoted to his cause, confesses before his death: "I never had time to look at things, Mac, never. I never looked how leaves come out. I never looked at the way things happen." It is an extraordinary exploration of mob mentality and tragic idealism. One of the characters, Doc Burton, a detached observer, is based on Ed Ricketts. Doc/Ricketts continues to appear in other Steinbeck novels, such as *Cannery Row* and *Sweet Thursday*. The opening quotation is from Milton's *Paradise Lost*:

> . . . What though the field be lost?
> All is not lost—the unconquerable will,
> And study of revenge, immortal hate,
> And courage never to submit or yield:
> And what is else not to be overcome?

The influence of *Paradise Lost* would also be felt later in Steinbeck's *The Grapes of Wrath*.

"SOMETHING THAT HAPPENED"

John and Carol Steinbeck had a small house built in the hills west of Los Gatos, about fifty miles north of Monterey. Carol's preoccupation with the house gave John the freedom to work on "Something that Happened," once again a story about farm workers struggling to retain their dignity. This was a simply-told tale of how their dreams, even the smallest ones, never seem to come true; how lonely they were even when surrounded by dozens of other workers; and how the phalanx can split even the relationship of two men who never should have been so close.

As Steinbeck turned "Something that Happened" into

a full-length novel, the characters began to grow and take on their own personalities through the dialogue he was writing. And it was just dialogue. There were no descriptive passages yet. More characters were introduced and through their introduction the plot was strengthened because each had a story to tell and each story became intertwined into the next character's story. The novel was developing exactly like a play, foreshadowing the dangers that the reader knows are there but must wait to see unfold.

Ed Ricketts suggested a new title: *Of Mice and Men* from "To a Mouse" by the Scottish poet Robert Burns: "the best laid schemes o' mice an' men gang aft a-gley/ [go often astray or awry] And leave us naught but grief and pain/For promised joy." Burns's poem talks about how humans cannot control the forces of nature, a topic in which Steinbeck and Ricketts were both interested. *Of Mice and Men* was completed in mid-August 1936. It took only two months to write the 30,000 words, and part of that was a rewrite: Steinbeck's dog Toby had chewed up the half-done manuscript. Steinbeck sent it off to Elizabeth Otis with a note in which he said that although he had faith in this short novel, he did not think it would have mass appeal.

OF MICE AND MEN

O*f Mice and Men* was the second most frequently banded book in the United States through the 1990s.[1] The narrative of the novel has roots in the legend of King Arthur—"the knightly loyalty, the pursuit of the vision, the creation of a bond and its destruction by an at least potentially adulterous relationship."[2] This novella was written very much like a play and was therefore very easy to adapt to the stage and to the screen. Like a play, the work is full of dialogue. And when there is description, it is not of the internal states of characters, but rather of their appearance or actions, or of sights, sounds, and physical details that surround them. The descriptions are very meticulous and almost like notes to a director and production designer.

GEORGE AND LENNIE

Chapter One establishes the relationship between the two main characters: George and Lennie. George is the loyal parallel to King Arthur. He is remarkably pure (he has no relations with women, even when the other workers go to the whorehouses). George is very critical of Curley's wife (perhaps because he senses her danger to Lennie) and of anything dirty that is exchanged between the men, such as when Curley boasts of keeping his hands in vaseline for his wife's sake.

The two bindlestiffs (hobos) are trying to make a life for themselves in California during the Depression. George is Lennie's protector, a fatherly figure looking after his grown child. Like a father, he scolds Lennie for misbehaving, and like a son, Lennie lives to please George. George must plan every moment of Lennie's life, because he is aware that Lennie cannot do it for himself. But he knows that no matter how carefully he plans, Lennie will do something foolish, and they will have to leave wherever they are and start life anew. George is tired of caring for Lennie and regrets that he must carry this burden with him wherever he goes. Yet he realizes that with Lennie to care for, he is not lonely like all the other migrant workers who, if they are lucky, find work, finish it and move on—always alone.

Lennie, on the other hand, is too simpleminded to think about his part of their relationship. Like a child, he is only concerned with what George can do for him. He cannot understand the broader aspects of life or its complexities, but can only remember small details, like raising rabbits. Ironically, Lennie is not dangerous because of his strength and size, but because of his innocence. For example, Lennie had no intention of harming the woman who claimed he attempted to rape her; he only wanted to feel her soft dress the same way he wanted to feel the soft mouse in his pocket that is now dead.

Lennie may be a gentle giant, but he has a capacity for great violence. For example, he complains to George during the description of the farm that he would kill any cat that hurt his rabbits. He submerges his violence because, as limited as he is, he understands that it is wrong. Thus, when Curley attacks him, he does not retaliate until George allows him to act. This incident foreshadows the terrible events at the end of the book.

IRONY—*The use of words to express an idea that is opposite to the words' literal meaning. (Example: When innocence is considered dangerous.)*

Being mildly retarded, Lennie's need for George is obvious. George's need for Lennie is more obscure, but no less intense. Lennie gives George a sense of power.[3] George directs Lennie, as perfectly illustrated in Lennie's fight with Curley. George is the brains and Lennie is the brawn. Lennie is what makes George special and gives him a reason for living.

FORESHADOW— *To hint at something that will happen later on in a story.*

Some critics have felt that Lennie was not human enough as a character. Others felt that "Lennie is not a character in the story at all, but rather a device like a golden coin in Moby Dick to which the other characters may react in a way that allows the reader to perceive their attitudes."[4]

CAIN AND ABEL

Of Mice and Men offers one of the first looks at Steinbeck's preoccupation with Biblical allegory. In this novel, George is cast as Cain and Lennie as Abel. It is somewhat of a revisionist look at the parable, wherein the goodness of Lennie is actually his feeble-minded innocence. Yet George volunteers to be his "brother's keeper"—he has been taking care of Lennie for years. He stays his brother's keeper to the end, when he shoots him—unlike Candy, who is too cowardly to put his dog out of its misery and Carlson has to do it. George wants to break the curse of Cain, to stop wandering the land and actually settle down.[5] In fact, the act of murder he performs upon his "brother" is an act of "keeping" him from the mob's destructive hands. He is a "good" Cain, because the murder he performs is not motivated by ill desires. "To empathize with Cain is to reevaluate what we call evil."[6] To Steinbeck, Abel is not totally good and Cain not totally evil. Steinbeck is particularly interested in redefining Cain's role in the relationship. This theme will reappear in future Steinbeck works, such as *The Grapes of Wrath* and, most notably, *East of Eden*.

THEME—*A distinctive quality or concern in one or more works of fiction.*

FORESHADOWING

Steinbeck foreshadows a number of things in this first chapter, to which he will return as the story continues:

George twice warns Lennie not to talk unnecessarily. Lennie carries a dead mouse in his pocket, too ashamed to tell George that he killed it, even though it is only a mouse. George finds a safe spot in which Lennie can hide because he knows Lennie will need it.

CANDY

When George and Lennie arrive at the bunkhouse, they meet Candy, the swamper (janitor). He is a weak, infirm old man who owns a weak, infirm old dog. Though he might seem nosy, Candy serves as the person who introduces George and Lennie to everyone on the farm. Candy is like a combination of an old Lennie and George. He is the only man on the farm who understands the relationship between George and Lennie because he has a similar relationship with his dog. The other men do not understand because their lives are not oriented toward caring. They, of necessity, must be survivors, men who must take care of only themselves. Candy knows he is useless and he has no future. He knows he is only kept at the ranch because he was injured there and because the boss expects that he will die soon. Like his dog, he is so handicapped that he is of little use. He knows his last chance to live out whatever years he has left is to latch onto George and become part of George's dream. He offers George money, thereby giving George hope of fulfilling his dream of buying a ranch.

CURLEY

Curley is the son of the ranch boss. Curley tries to incite Lennie as soon as he first meets him. Candy explains that Curley is jealous of big men and will fight them so if he loses he can claim it was their size, not their ability that caused him to lose. George explains to Candy that though Lennie is big, he does not know anything about fighting. While playing cards, Candy tells them that Curley was married a few weeks ago and since then has been wearing a glove over a hand covered in Vaseline to keep his hand soft for his wife, whom Candy accuses of being a "tart." Soon after, George, who suddenly seems frightened, warns Lennie to keep away from Curley, and again reminds him where to hide if he gets into trouble.

Curley appears as the antagonist, the threat to everyone on the ranch when, in fact, he is the most insecure. Not only is he physically small but he also knows he cannot sexually satisfy his wife and at any minute she could be with any one of the workers. He wears boots with large heels to make him appear taller and to make him feel bigger. He realizes that by fighting Lennie, he can gain some respect from his farmhands. His wife—the only female character without a name—is indeed a tramp. It is obvious that she cares about her appearance not for her husband but to entice the other men. And Curley knows it—why else would he be constantly searching for her? Through George's reaction when he first sees her, the reader is immediately aware that she is a threat to both Lennie and George.

CURLEY'S WIFE

Curley's wife walks in looking for her husband. She is the lady in red: dress, shoes, lipstick, and fingernails. And she sensually teases the men before she leaves. George cannot deny her beauty and her allure but immediately senses what she is up to and warns Lennie to stay away from her. He knows she is more trouble than either one of them can handle. Her confrontation with the three "weak men" reveals that she knows that men dislike her. But she blames it on male insecurity. Men, she claims, are only able to attack her when they come together. Together, as a phalanx, men are strong, but as individuals, men only think of themselves. She is extremely lonely, but she realizes that the men are also lonely: their favorite escape is a whorehouse in the town of Soledad, the Spanish word for "solitude."

PUPPIES

Slim enters the bunkhouse to tell Curley's wife that he saw Curley on his way home and to announce that the night before his dog had a litter of nine puppies, but he drowned four of them because his dog couldn't nurse all nine. Carlson, a big burly man, comes in to meet the new men and asks Slim to give one pup to Candy because his dog is so old and feeble that it should be put down out of sympathy. Lennie, of course, wants a pup too and George tells him he will try to get one for him. Curley returns and asks George if he has seen his wife. George replies that he saw her about half an hour before looking for Curley.

The relationship between Lennie and George is an oddity to everyone at the farm, but especially to the boss who cannot possibly believe that two men could be so strongly attached unless they were blood relatives. Although George considers himself and Lennie an insep-arable duo, throughout the first few chapters George plays solitaire to amuse himself. Lennie's sacrifice of his own life so George could survive is mirrored in Slim's need to kill four of the pups so that the other five can live. Slim is the most intelligent of all the farm hands and under-stands what motivates the others.

WOMEN IN THE NOVEL

Most of the women in the novel are viewed in a negative light. For example, when the topic of Curley's wife comes up, Whit, a farmhand, suggests they all go to a whore-house in town that night. There are two available: one run by old Susy, the other by Clara. The fact that the whore-house madam has the same name as Aunt Clara, who reared Lennie until her death, associates the Aunt with impropriety. There is also the young girl from Weed, who accused Lennie of raping her, when all he wanted to do was touch her dress. Her accusation launches a lynch mob, from which George and Lennie barely escape.

Women in this novel lead to no good. They do not seem to understand and are quick to jump to conclusions, which can set off deadly forces. The perfect example of this is Curley's wife, whom Steinbeck has not named at all. She is dangerous and association with her leads to tragedy.

LIVING LIES

All the characters in the novel are living lies. Curley knows his marriage will never work out but will not admit it. His wife knows there never was a show business career for her, but she will continue to tell the story at the drop of a hat. George knows that he will never have a farm of his own, but he keeps talking himself and Lennie into it. And Candy knows his dog cannot live without his constant care and that he also needs constant care to survive.

CROOKS

Crooks is introduced in Chapter Four. Crooks shows his bitterness by isolating himself in his room and not allowing anyone to come in. If he cannot be accepted by the white world, then the white world is not invited into his home. But Lennie is also an outsider and Crooks comes to like him. He allows Lennie to enter his room. It is not surprising that, later in the chapter, he does not forbid Candy from entering. Is Candy not as much of an outcast as he? In truth, Crooks would like to live in the main bunkhouse with all the other men.

When Crooks tries to have Lennie imagine what it would be like without George, he is actually trying to explain his own loneliness, his own isolation, his own rejection by white people. But because he is a pragmatist, he is forced to tell Lennie that the dream he shares with George is a foolish one. However, when Candy makes the plan sound plausible, his deep need to be accepted allows him to bid for a job. Of course, Candy is as much of a dreamer as Lennie and Crooks.

ACCIDENTS

As George predicts, Lennie kills the puppy. Though it was an accident, it still shows that Lennie cannot control his anger. In fact, he becomes even angrier at the pup for being so fragile. Lennie is upset because he fears George's punishment, not because he feels bad for killing. Curley's wife comes upon him and the two almost arrive at a moment of understanding. Through dual conversations—Lennie about the farm and rabbits and she about her truncated show business life—their ideas merge with a discussion of the touch of soft objects, like rabbits, velvet, and her hair. Curley's wife calls Lennie "nuts" but counters with "you're a kinda nice fella. Jus' like a big baby." She invites Lennie to feel her hair. But when he lingers too long she claims he will "muss it." Lennie can't let go and in a moment of panic, while covering her mouth to keep her from screaming, breaks her neck.

MERCY KILLING

As soon as George sees the body, he knows exactly what has happened and how to deal with it. He realizes it is senseless to deny Lennie's guilt and knows that he will die a horrible death when the men get their hands on him. Candy must fight for his own life when he asks George if there is still a chance the two of them could buy a farm. At this point George finally verbalizes the truth—there never was a chance. He tells the men that Lennie must have gone south, then goes to Carlson's bunk and steals his gun.

As Lennie waits for George down by the Salinas River, he is not concerned that he has killed a person. He is distraught over what George will think of him and if he will be told to go off on his own. He suffers a psychotic episode with hallucinations. He envisions his Aunt Clara as an overbearing shrew who scolds him for his wrongdoing. This implies that while Lennie was growing up, Aunt Clara may have been very strict and perhaps cruel. Then a huge rabbit appears. Throughout the novel, the rabbit has been a symbol of the gentle side of Lennie, but now it is an ogre and it torments Lennie with vile threats. When George comes, Lennie urges George to recite the continuing litany about their relationship being unique and about the farm and the rabbits. George calms Lennie by telling him about the farm and then shoots him in the back of the head in much the same way Slim shot Candy's dog. As Candy should have shot his own dog, George knew it was his place to shoot Lennie. It was a mercy killing. George then tells the others that he shot Lennie in self-defense with Carlson's stolen pistol.

COMING FULL CIRCLE

George undergoes a great change. Though he has constantly told Lennie that he would be happier without him, George always knew that he was incomplete without his buddy. They were like two parts of one being: Lennie, the body, and George, the brains. As much as George complained about Lennie, he actually valued and needed his friendship to feel important. Without Lennie there is no dream of a farm. When George tells Lennie about living without him, just before he pulls the trigger, the speech is delivered without emotion because George knows that this time it is a lie. George does not want to be a solitary figure—but now he must. Lennie is dead and so is the dream and so is a part of George. Slim immediately knows what really happened, but the others are bewildered about why George is so disturbed about the shooting.

There is a circular structure in the novel, a neat balance between the opening and closing scenes. In the opening scene, George and Lennie climb down to the pool from the highway. And in the closing scene, George and Slim climb up from the pool to the highway. By losing Lennie, George becomes just like any other man, "destroying the thing that makes him different and reducing himself to the status of an ordinary guy."[7] However, this tragedy offers a glimmer of hope. George is not walking off a total loner—he is walking off with Slim. Just two ordinary men walking off, but together. There is a bond between them—it is prescribed in the circular structure of the novel. Both Slim and George are very understanding men, and they are sensitive to what has just happened. They are not fictional dreamers, the kind George pretended to be for Lennie's sake. Perhaps their dream of owning a farm is more realizable now that they have formed a phalanx and accepted their status as average men.

WRITING THE FIRST "BIG BOOK"

After *Of Mice and Men* was finished, Steinbeck had time to accept an assignment to write a series of articles about migrant workers for the *San Francisco News*. He was to visit the various regions to observe living and working conditions. He was particularly interested in seeing how the government-run camps were helping the migrants. In order not to be too conspicuous, Steinbeck bought a bakery truck and outfitted it with bedding, cooking utensils, and all the other items he would need for his trip. Steinbeck was shocked to see the cardboard boxes and abandoned water viaducts in which whole families lived. Because food was so scarce and so expensive, people were forced to eat stray dogs and cats and even rodents. At this time, such horrific sights were far from rare in the Central Valley.

By 1936, it was reported that nearly 90,000 Okies (as migrant share croppers and workers from small farms who came from any of the dust bowl states were called) had moved to California hoping to find work or some land. Until then, little was said about the unfair treatment of the workers because most were Chinese, Japanese, Filipino, or Mexican. But when statistics proved that because of the migration west the majority of starving migrants were white Americans, the press decided to intervene.[1] And even then there was a racist undertone not only in the *News* but also in Steinbeck's own comments. The *News* editorial that appeared with one of the articles in his series said that the farmhands who had migrated from the dust bowl "are Americans of old stock. . . .They cannot be handled as the Japanese, Mexicans and Filipinos." Steinbeck wrote: "Farm labor in California will be white Labor, it will be American labor, and it will insist on a standard of living much higher than that which was accorded the foreign 'cheap labor.'" He went on to say that these migrants "will refuse to accept the role of field peons, with attendant terrorism, squalor and starvation." But those who spent their lives in the dust bowl considered themselves farmers and were not as interested in unionizing, as were the Mexicans and Filipinos of the early 1930s.[2]

So here they were, mainly Bible-belt fundamentalist Christians, leaving behind a homeland devastated by the Depression and drought, trying to find nonexistent jobs, accused of being ignorant, dirty, and immoral, blockaded by border police, verbally battered, and physically abused. It made perfect sense that conflict between the native

Californians and the migrants would occur. Locals resisted allowing migrants into town for fear that the children of those in the camps would overcrowd the schools, or absorb more than their share of relief funds, and that union organizing would interfere with local government. One community refused to allow "Negroes and Okies" to sit anywhere except the theater balcony.[3]

Those who lived in squatters' camps survived, barely, under foul conditions. Those on farms were not much better off, but they were given a piece of land on which to pitch a tent and park a vehicle. A spigot and an outhouse were made available to them. Those who were lucky enough to find harvesting jobs on larger farms lived in one-room shacks for which they were charged a fee, ate food that had to be bought from a company store at inflated prices, and shared a shower and toilet with two hundred other Okies.

In contrast to these appalling sites were the fifteen governments camps, known as "sanitary camps," three of which could be moved around the area in case of emergencies. During August 1936, Steinbeck visited what he called "rotten and deplorable" places owned by farmers who would not use the government models that were very successful at maintaining sanitary and safe conditions for the workers. While at the Arvin Sanitary Camp, Steinbeck met Tom Collins, a sanitary camp manager at "Weedpatch," as those who lived in Arvin called it. Steinbeck was impressed with how well the camp was run. He was even more impressed with Collins who, no matter how tired he might have been, knew what was going on at all times in every corner of his camp. Collins, at one time, began studying for the priesthood but switched to teaching in Guam and Alaska and then founded a school for delinquent teens in San Francisco. From there he went on to aid the homeless in a program established by the Roosevelt administration. In 1935 he accepted a position in the Resettlement Administration as the first manager of a sanitary camp. As manager, he created a system in which the residents governed themselves and were permitted to make camp rules and enforce them.

Before Steinbeck got back into the "pie wagon" (as he called his bakery truck), Collins gave him reams of reports, notes, case studies, and observations that all fed his *News* articles. He even included lyrics to camp songs and notes on the dialects of the migrants—invaluable reference material. Before returning home to Los Gatos, Steinbeck stopped in Salinas and was shocked to see how terrible conditions were there. A strike by lettuce pickers had created enormous hostility between the farmworkers and the town businessmen. There were attempted attacks on the camps and people were forbidden from walking the streets after dark. The police, however, kept out of the conflict.

When he finally got back to Los Gatos, Steinbeck wrote to Tom Collins to tell him how impressed he was with the experience of visiting the camp and he hoped that the articles he was about to write would help to show the plight of the downtrodden. He enclosed a sizable check to be used by the migrants for raising cattle. His plan also was to send books for the children to encourage them to learn to read.

Steinbeck's first article on the migrants appeared in the *Nation* on September 12, 1936. He then completed the seven articles that were commissioned for publication from October 5 through 11 by the *San Francisco News*. They were then expanded and released in a bound edition called *Starvation Under the Orange Trees* and later retitled *The Harvest Gypsies*. Each article was as objective as Steinbeck could make it. He knew that if he began grandstanding, he would cause some to become angry and his campaign for better conditions would be doomed. But it did not matter. Some took exception to the material; others asked him to lecture about the camps. In several letters and conversations after the publication of *The Harvest Gypsies*, Steinbeck expressed his fear that the destitution and unfairness of the migrant workers' conditions might push them to violence and even lead to a civil war of sorts. He felt the situation was very dangerous.

Meanwhile, *Of Mice and Men* was also generating interest. The Book of the Month Club named the book its main selection, guaranteeing substantial sales. It appeared in February 1937 and within a few weeks sold 117,000 copies. Most critics thought highly of "the little book," as Steinbeck referred to it.[4]

Annie Laurie Williams, who handled film and stage contracts for McIntosh and Otis, had shown *Of Mice and*

Men to Beatrice Kaufman who was the East Coast representative for Samuel Goldwyn Pictures. She, in turn, passed the novel on to her husband, George S. Kaufman, the noted playwright and director, who saw immediately that Steinbeck had written this novel in play form. He brought Sam Harris on board as producer and the two of them planned a stage production for the following fall. But the Steinbecks had already planned an extensive trip to Europe. John did some preliminary writing with Kaufman but when April 15 arrived, the Steinbecks boarded a freighter and set sail. In Europe, he discovered, he was well-known. The Steinbecks' visit to Russia was enlightening and disheartening at the same time. John did not enjoy being considered a spokesman for the American working class. He realized it was easy to see that the treatment of the poor farmworkers in America was no different from the way Russia treated all of its citizens.[5]

When the Steinbecks returned to New York, John knew he had to get the play ready. But he was reluctant because he had never written a play before and he was eager to begin a new book about the migrant workers. Annie Laurie Williams, experienced with scripts, taught him playwriting style and Kaufman invited him to spend a week on his farm in Pennsylvania to finish it. Once done, Steinbeck waited for casting to be completed and then left for California.

John and Carol decided to drive back home. They bought a red Chevrolet in New York and once they passed

Chicago, they followed Route 66 through Oklahoma right back to California, the same route the Okies followed. Once home, Steinbeck set out to join Tom Collins again. When he finally met up with Collins, they spent three weeks working in the field in the Gridley area and then went on to the squatters' camp, but Steinbeck told everyone they had gone to Oklahoma to trace the routes of the migrants. By November 7, stockpiled with notes based on the experiences he had with Collins, they returned to Los Gatos to a huge surprise party thrown by Carol.

The *Of Mice and Men* opening night on Broadway was November 23, 1937. The critical response was positive and the audiences enjoyed it enough to keep the play running for 207 performances. The New York Drama Critics Circle, choosing it over Thornton Wilder's *Our Town* by twelve to four, voted it the Best American Play of 1938. It was cited for, among other things, "its refusal to make this study of tragic loneliness and frustration either cheap or sensational."[6]

Celebrity status began to take its toll. Steinbeck was suddenly besieged with requests for charity, handouts, and donations. Some were legitimate, like helping Ed Ricketts pay off the loans he took out to rebuild Pacific Biologicals after it burned down a few years earlier. He was even involved in a phony paternity suit to extort money from him. Worst of all, Carol seemed to begrudge John's success. She resented that after all these years she had nothing to show for herself. Although she was responsible for turning some pretty sloppy writing into good manuscripts, she never published anything of note. Now what the couple shared most was quarrelling. Rather than attempt to reconcile the difficulties, Steinbeck did exactly what he did when he felt the pressure of his parents' illnesses and encroaching poverty. He hid himself away and wrote.

As he worked on his new novel that he satirically called *L'Affaire Lettuceberg*, his heart was not in it. He saw it as a way of fictionalizing his phalanx theory, but clearly it did not work in this novel. However, Steinbeck was too disturbed over the mistreatment of the migrants to be able to think clearly and approach the book from another direction. He longed to be back at the camps to try to do what little he could to help the migrant farmers. He was horrified that five thousand families were starving to death and no one with any power cared enough to help. "In one tent," he told Elizabeth Otis, "there are twenty people quarantined for smallpox and two of the women are to have babies in that tent this week."[7] Steinbeck wanted to use some of his Hollywood money that he was receiving for his work on *Of Mice and Men* to give $2 apiece to three thousand migrant workers. The local people feared that the workers would grow too strong and begin to organize again, so they blocked whatever food and medicine was coming in. But, Steinbeck argued, if these migrants were not in California, the crops could never be harvested because without them there would not be enough men to do the work. Nevertheless, California refused any relief to the migrant workers because they were not citizens of the state and by law were not entitled to it. Moreover, Social Security, unemployment insurance, the minimum wage, and the National Labor Relations Act did not cover agricultural workers.

Conditions became worse when heavy rain struck the Visalia area and continued for weeks, flooding the land so badly that people were sleeping on soaked blankets in flooded tents. Children developed pneumonia and died. Though the Farm Security Administration attempted to help by providing food, medicine, and clothing, the mud was so deep they could hardly get through. Steinbeck spent two weeks with Collins at Weedpatch, bringing food to the farmworkers, tending to their illnesses, and simply dragging people out of the rain to shelter under trees. He returned home to an assignment from *Life* magazine to document the atrocities with Horace Bristol, a photographer. Steinbeck told Elizabeth Otis if she could get *Life* to print the articles he would use the money to pay for medicine because he could not, in good conscience, make any money based on the migrants' pain. But once completed, the article was turned down by *Life* because the editors demanded that the style be softened and the language toned down, which Steinbeck refused to do. They also considered the piece "too liberal."[8]

Disappointed and dejected, Steinbeck returned to Los Gatos and again threw himself into working on his novel. *L'Affaire Lettuceberg* was finished in April. Covici-Friede was on the verge of bankruptcy and wanted to publish it immediately, thinking it would save the company. But after Steinbeck reread the pages, he hated it. Carol hated it too and advised John to burn it. As guilty as he felt about hurting Pat Covici, there was nothing he could do but actually burn the manuscript.

In mid-May Steinbeck opened a brand-new ledger and began writing a brand-new book, "the big book." He had to tell the world about the plight of the migrant workers and if no one would publish his articles, he would tell his story in the way he new best: a novel that would focus on the simple, good people who were thrown into a grueling situation beyond their control. Perhaps then the public would learn what was going on. Perhaps then someone would help.

Steinbeck worked methodically each day, building slowly until the writing seemed to soar. By October, he had written two hundred thousand words. The summer was filled with interruptions such as visits from family, friends, and celebrities like Charlie Chaplin and Broderick Crawford. There were also requests for radio appearances and the purchase of the Biddle Ranch. John and Carol had returned to the same confusion they went through when they moved to Los Gatos while John was working on *Of Mice and Men*. Nevertheless, they had a new house built and the old house remodeled on a piece of property five miles from town. As a gift to Carol, John had a pool installed with a brass plate affixed to the diving board dedicating the pool to her. About the same time as the foundation was being poured on the new house, Carol came up with the title of the new book. They agreed it was perfect: *The Grapes of Wrath*.

Then there was Carol's bout with strep throat and the subsequent removal of her tonsils. Still, by December 1938, John and Carol had finished revising the manuscript. Carol was far more than just a typist. As she worked, she corrected grammar and syntax and rewrote awkward passages. She was Steinbeck's editor before Pat Covici received the manuscript. So grateful was John that the dedication to the book reads, in part: "To Carol, who willed this book."

But at that moment, Covici was in trouble. His bankruptcy could easily have ended his career in publishing and could have been harmful to Steinbeck as well. Being bankrupt, Covici's assets could have been claimed by the printer. That money included Steinbeck's royalties. John was immediately emotionally thrown back to his early days of poverty and he became concerned. He had a contract with Covici for five more novels. In order to break the contract he sent Covici five novels over the next five weeks that were nothing more than hand-written pages of total gibberish and demanded his advance. That quickly solved the problem. Because Steinbeck was such a valuable commodity, Covici was able to get a job at the prestigious Viking Press by guaranteeing he would bring Steinbeck with him. Viking paid Steinbeck the royalties Covici owed him and, in addition, guaranteed the September publication of *The Long Valley*, a collection of short stories. These were stories that had appeared in first, and then as the central ribs of strength grew weak, each leaf tilted downward. Then it was June, and the sun shone more fiercely. The brown lines on the corn leaves widened and moved in on the central ribs. The weeds frayed and ~~moved~~ edged back toward their roots. The air was thin and the sky more pale; and every day the earth paled.

In the roads where the teams moved, where the wheels milled the ground and the hooves of the horses beat the ground, the dirt crust broke and the dust formed. Every moving thing lifted the dust into the air; a walking man lifted a ~~cloud~~ thin layer as high as his waist, and a wagon lifted the dust as high as the fence tops, and an automobile boiled a cloud behind it. The dust was long in settling back again.

When June was half gone, the big clouds moved up out of Texas and the gulf, high heavy clouds, rain-heads. The men

A page from Steinbeck's lengthy manuscript of *The Grapes of Wrath*, typewritten by Carol Steinbeck. The handwritten notations are the personal edits of Steinbeck, himself.

major magazines between 1933 and 1937. The book also included the first complete version of *The Red Pony*.

The Red Pony, set on a ranch in the Salinas Valley, is comprised of four different sections that share characters, settings, and themes. It is Jody's coming-of-age story, in which the pony functions as a symbol of both innocence and maturing. Steinbeck's childhood pony, Jill, was the inspiration for this work.[9]

While visiting at Los Gatos, Covici read a portion of *The Grapes of Wrath* and knew immediately that Steinbeck had written a masterpiece. He planned an enormous first printing. Steinbeck disagreed and wrote to Elizabeth Otis to restrain Covici from getting carried away over the number of books. He thought that many people would object to his ideas and the book might not sell, putting Covici's position at Viking in jeopardy. But Covici was right. The advance sale of *The Grapes of Wrath* passed 90,000 by the April release date— an extremely impressive number.

The next battle was over the language. Steinbeck had spent a great deal of time joining the authentic vocabulary, even if it was raw, and the speech patterns of the migrants to rhythms he created (based on actual classical music) as a style for the book. Viking, however, could not care less. They demanded the language be cleaned up. Elizabeth Otis came out to Los Gatos and together with Carol, coaxed John into modifying the sometimes obscene language so the book could go forward. Steinbeck stood firm on some of the language, such as the word "shit-heels," for example, but relented on most. After a contentious two days, Carol telegraphed in the changes to Viking.

Once the language issue was settled, Viking expressed dissatisfaction with the ending. The editors thought it was anticlimactic, especially after the power of the sections before it. But Steinbeck refused to change a word and Viking finally agreed.

There were still problems. For one, Steinbeck was a physical wreck. After some tests that indicated he had neuritis and that his metabolism was extremely low, he was confined to bed for a few weeks. The bombardment of these physical ailments coupled with the strain of completing the novel began to cause him emotional problems that led to fears of real and imagined intimidation. He received threats from rightwing groups because of his defense of the migrant workers and even negative comments from leftists who did not think he portrayed the farm workers honestly and accurately. He had heard rumors that J. Edgar Hoover, head of the FBI, was investigating him, and that the Associated Farmers organization was claiming he was a Communist. He even believed that the paternity suit that had been filed against him the year before was a trumped up charge to smear him. He began to imagine that he and Carol could possibly be in danger.[10] And the book had yet to be published.

Things happened very quickly once *The Grapes of Wrath* was published. The first printing was almost twenty thousand copies, all issued as first editions. They were quickly sold and by May 17 there were 83,000 copies in circulation. It remained a best-seller for more than a year with a total of 429,000 copies sold by the end of 1939. The film rights sold for $75,000, an extremely high fee at that time for a novel to be adapted into a screenplay.[11]

THE RESPONSE

In April the first reviews of *The Grapes of Wrath* began to appear. As usual, some critics claimed the writing was "sentimental" and others called it "superficial," especially in regard to the ending. Some were annoyed by the

INTERCALARY—
Something inserted between two things or parts.

intercalary chapters breaking the flow of the narrative that, moreover, were didactic and moralizing. Others thought they made the story of the Joads more universal, showing what life was like all around them through impersonal commentary.

The *New Yorker* critic Clifton Fadiman thought, "the ending is the tawdriest kind of fake symbolism," but added, "If only a couple of million overcomfortable people can be brought to read it, John Steinbeck's *The Grapes of Wrath* may actually effect something like a revolution in their minds and hearts."[12] By and large, *The Grapes of Wrath* was a success. Charles Angoff of *The National Review* compared Steinbeck's contribution to literature to that of Melville, Hawthorne, Crane, and Norris. He believed "the book had all the earmarks of something momentous, monumental, and memorable."[13] A review in the April 17 issue of *Time* magazine claimed, "This is John Ernst Steinbeck's longest novel (619 pages) and his best novel, i.e., his toughest and tenderest, his roughest written and most mellifluous, his most realistic and, in its ending, his most melodramatic, his angriest and most idyllic. It is 'great' in the way that *Uncle Tom's Cabin* was great because it is inspired propaganda, half tract, half human interest story, emotionalizing a great theme."[14]

Although *The Grapes of Wrath* is fiction, many people responded to it as a piece of journalism. The book was banned in cities across the country, as political propaganda, scathing, and even pornography. Archbishop

Francis Spellman attacked it in the Hearst newspapers. A congressman from Oklahoma took exception to how the Okies were depicted and wanted the book banned in his state. The Oklahoma Chamber of Commerce attempted to prohibit the movie from being made.

A small book, *Grapes of Gladness: California's Refreshing and Inspiring Answer to John Steinbeck's 'Grapes of Wrath'* began circulating. It was the story of a poor midwestern family that came to Southern California and found the Garden of Eden. They were welcomed by landowners, bankers, local people and loaned money to begin their new life and free land to cultivate. Then there was another book, *The Truth About John Steinbeck and the Migrants*, which told about how the author disguised himself as a migrant worker, was able to earn about four dollars a day, and was invited to live in the ranch house throughout the year.

Those who defended the book now took up arms. Learned scholars and professionals who knew the conditions in the camps touted its accuracy. The radio program *Town Meeting* debated the issues raised in the novel. When it realized the impact of *The Grapes of Wrath*, *Life* magazine decided it was time to publish the piece Steinbeck had been begging them to print. Their pages were filled with Horace Bristol's harrowing photographs. Even Darryl Zanuck, who was to produce the film based on the novel, sent a team of men to the farm areas to investigate if Steinbeck was telling the truth. They reported back that conditions were actually much worse than he had written.

THE
GRAPES
OF WRATH

Although *The Grapes of Wrath* is more about the pursuit of self-fulfillment than it is about injustice or migration, the book is still considered a protest novel. The novel essentially has three parts: the devastation, the journey, and the destination. The devastation ends at chapter 10; the journey ends at chapter 18; the destination completes the book. Using a correlation between this novel and the Old Testament, these three divisions parallel the Jewish oppression in Egypt, the Exodus, and the arrival in Canaan.

Philosophically, the novel combines the American influences of Emerson's concept of the transcendental oversoul, Protestant pragmatism and self-reliance, Whitman's love for every man and democracy, and Jefferson's agrarianism.

A further breakdown is the use of alternating intercalary chapters, or "interchapters." These sixteen short chapters take up less than one hundred pages, just one-sixth of the novel. They diverge from the narrative and express Steinbeck's ideas about migration, equality,

PROTEST NOVEL—*A novel with a message about a current social or political condition and calls for change.*

weather, socialization, unscrupulous car salesmen, and other topics vital to understanding the migrant workers and their social conditions. Each of these impersonal interchapters links to the personal life of the Joads in the next chapter. Each is written in its own style, sometimes biblical, sometimes narrative, sometimes editorial, sometimes using a clipped rhythm, sometimes a flowing lilt—each one appropriate to the subject matter. Steinbeck's alternating styles "suggest a number of influences—the Bible, Dos Passos' 'Newsreel' technique, folk idiom, Walt Whitman, Hemingway, and perhaps Carl Sandburg's *The People, Yes.*"[1] Some subjects are trivial, but Steinbeck's technique elevates them to greater importance. A very famous previous use of interchapters is by Tolstoy in *War and Peace*. The variety of styles used in the interchapters prevents them from being clumped in a group, thereby splitting *The Grapes of Wrath* in two: the narrative and the non-narrative. Ironically, by refusing to blend in, each interchapter's individuality contributes to the cohesiveness of the novel as a whole.

Another technique Steinbeck uses to maintain the coherence of his epic novel is the interweaving of symbols. For example, the images of dust, the turtle, and the red ant, just to name a few, appear throughout the book.

THE PERSONALIZED GROUP

Some critics have felt that Steinbeck's characters are not realistic. Other critics have maintained that in order to show the universal plight of man, Steinbeck was purposefully trying to create mythic or representational characters. Many cite the preface of *The Forgotten Village* as the explanation:

> A great many documentary films have used the generalized method, that is, the showing of a condition or an event as it affects a group of people . . . [but] it means very little to know that a million Chinese are starving unless you know one Chinese who is starving . . . Our story is centered on one family . . . Then, from association with this little personalized group, the larger conclusion concerning the racial group could be drawn with something like participation.[2]

Thereby, the one family Steinbeck uses can represent more than just its personal situation. Behind that family's actions are those of thousands who are in the same predicament. That is one way of looking at why Steinbeck's characters sometimes feel unreal or larger than life.

THE DROUGHT

Steinbeck does not begin the novel with the narrative. Instead, he sets the scene on an epic scale. The first chapter is an interchapter, since none of the main characters appear, and there are no plot points. Nothing "happens." The first chapter is analogous to the first slow sweeping shots in a movie that establish the scene and paint the landscape for the viewer. Chapter one describes the drought: the dust is so thick that people have covered their faces with handkerchiefs and wear goggles to protect their eyes. The corn crop lies dead beneath a shroud of dust. No one in the Oklahoma dust bowl seems to know what to do. The cadences of the lines and their phraseology are notable: they seem to be right out of the Bible. Steinbeck creates a sense of despair on a biblical scale in a manner reminiscent of the plagues on the Egyptians. This prepares the reader for a story of mythic proportions.

TOM JOAD

Tom Joad is introduced in the second chapter, as he hitchhikes home from jail. He was released early for good behavior, he tells the driver of the truck who picks him up. Although the truck with its "No Riders" sign is a manifestation of the corporate conglomerate, the driver is only human, just like Tom. He's bored and that is why he picks up a hitchhiker. Tom and the driver find common ground, agreeing on their dislike of the rich and those who pontificate. They believe only a preacher can use big words. Others who do just get them confused. Tom is presented as a likable, bright individual, although he is not educated. He later gives his views on rehabilitation: prisons do not

Dust storms forced the abandonment of many farms during the 1930s, including the one above near Liberal, Kansas.

rehabilitate men, but there is no other way. The irony is that prison, for the poor, can be a safe haven guaranteeing food and shelter. It is the outside world that is not so secure.

SYMBOLS

A turtle slowly crawls across the road and is barely missed by a car. Then a truck comes by and one of its wheels whisks the rim of the turtle shell, tipping it over and forcing it back to the roadside. With great effort, the turtle rights itself. Steinbeck sees the turtle as the farmworker who goes about his business bothering no one, but is in constant jeopardy. The turtle is also symbolic of the Joads, heading to the Southwest, ready to pick themselves up when something knocks them down. The turtle carries its half-shell of a house, much like Wink Manley, who split a house with the Joads. The truck is again a symbol of the wealthy people in big business who have no regard for the poor farmworker. The turtle foreshadows the life the Joads will lead— plodding along on their own, only to be continuously knocked over by the corporate world. Tom picks up the turtle and carries it with him for his younger brother. Jim Casy, a former minister, reminds him that one cannot keep a turtle; it must go off on its own when it needs to, much like Tom Joad.

The grapes are both a symbol of abundance and of anger. Both meanings exist in the Bible. In the novel, Grampa daydreams about the prosperity that awaits them in California: "Gonna get me a whole big bunch a grapes off a bush, or whatever an' I'm gonna squash 'em on my face an' let 'em run offen my chin." Yet, grapes can also rot, especially if no one harvests them. As it states in an interchapter: "In the souls of the people the grapes of wrath are filling and growing heavy, heavy for the vintage."

California represents the Garden of Eden, a symbol Steinbeck had used before. Consider Lennie and George dreaming of the farm they are going to own someday.

JIM CASY

Jim and Tom discuss Jim's religion and the sexual experiences he had with young women he had converted. Along the way he concludes that perhaps what he did was not a sin, but just what humans do. Jim Casy is the voice for Steinbeck's religious viewpoint. His initials are those of Jesus Christ. Like Christ, he will sacrifice himself for Tom and then for others. He is part preacher, part philosopher, and part sage who is not tethered to religious dogma. At first he felt guilty by his physical attraction to the women he converted to Christianity, but in time he realized that there is no vice or virtue, there's "just stuff people do." We are all part of the Holy Spirit, Jim claims, connected by one common soul. That is one of the principles of Transcendentalism, an American philosophy espoused by the likes of Emerson, Thoreau, and Walt Whitman. Jim Casy feels he has lost his connection to Jesus, but retained his faith in common folks as the personification of God. When the Joads invite Casy to say grace over dinner, Casy explains to the family that he cannot because he has lost his faith and has gone off into the wilderness just as

TRANSCENDENTALISM— *The term Transcendentalism comes from the word "transcend," which means "to go beyond." Transcendentalism taught that man was basically good and that human life went beyond the experiences of the physical world.*

Christ did. All he is sure of is that when people are together as one, they are holy, but when someone runs off, he breaks the holiness, though he is not sure what it really means to be holy.

Twice, in Chapter 18, Casy discusses things he does not understand: once is when he speaks of the greed of the wealthy and the second time when he tells Sairy that he prays but he has lost God. She assures him he has not; he just cannot see him.

Casy's behavior is Christ-like as he sacrifices himself to save Tom. Casy is arrested instead of Tom because Casy knows Tom is in violation of parole and would face severe punishment. As he is driven off, Casy smiles. He has become the martyr, giving of himself for another.

In jail, Casy learns the lesson of strength in numbers. One person complaining about spoiled beans was not enough, but when all the prisoners protested, a phalanx was created. And it rose up against the prison.

When Casy is released from jail, he begins organizing strikes. Casy has found his calling. If he could not herd his flock in the ministry, he has found a way to do it through civil disobedience. When Casy is attacked, once again we hear, "You don't know what you're doing." Coincidentally, he is killed in the river, perhaps referring to Christ at the River Jordan. This time he is truly a martyr. Tom avenges his death and must go into hiding before he reemerges as a disciple.

Big Business

Chapter 5, the third interchapter, is written as a mock dialogue between two non-existent people. This vocal dramatization of a philosophical argument is reminiscent of the use of a chorus in a Greek tragedy. This interchapter talks about the monsters encroaching on the earth. It reveals that one tractor can do the job of a dozen farm families, so the tenant farmers on bank-financed land are told that they are no longer necessary. The bank representatives who have no interest in the farmers and no desire to be there come to evict them and it is all so impersonal. The next intruders are the tractors that Steinbeck describes as the earth's violators. Like the bank representatives, the tractors come without feeling for people or the land. They just do their job. If the farmers retaliate, there is no one to fight. They are not battling a person; they are not even battling a tractor; they are battling a bank. The bankers are more destructive than the dust that destroys the crops. These monsters are totally devoid of human emotions and though the bankers purport to be there to help finance the land, Steinbeck tells us in truth they are looking for quick monetary returns at the expense of destroying the soil. He goes on to describe the onslaught of tractors that cut into the land like surgery and violate it like rape. But the men who represent the banks and the men who drive the tractors are the same: they are merely doing their jobs in order to feed their families, much the same as the farmworkers are doing. They cannot be blamed.

In Chapter 7, another interchapter, a car salesmen tries to make a better deal by looking at customers' weaknesses to take advantage of them. He sells jalopies rather than new cars or quality used cars. Car dealers are like big business everywhere. They exploit the poor. A new car or a good used car does not reap as much of a profit as a wreck under the hood that appears to be in good condition. That is a good sale. The writing style of this interchapter changes to brisk sentences in the manner of a salesman trying to make a quick deal.

Casy makes a remark about there being something worse than the devil, presumably referring to capitalist society. And though Steinbeck's characters allow that no one can be blamed for trying to earn a living, there is no acknowledgment that modern technology must continue, inevitably causing some to lose jobs while new jobs are created. Perhaps it is because these folks are so much a part of the land that they have never seen it necessary to find a newer or better way to farm. It was the way their grandparents farmed, their parents farmed, and now the way they farm. For Al, fixing Mr. Wilson's car is easy.

Would it not be just as easy for him to fix a tractor? Presumably not, since the tractor is evil. If that is true, then is not the car evil too? Yet the car is liberating them and taking them to Eden. Are they better off in bondage, shackled to dead land? Is Grampa's death a metaphor for his being torn from the soil and therefore no longer being able to live? Or is it a signal that as we evolve into a more technical (and capitalist controlled) society, we must make room for those who will grow with us and eliminate those who will not?

METAPHOR—*A figure of speech in which a comparison is made between two words or phrases that have no literal relationship.*

LAND

People in *The Grapes of Wrath* have ties to their land and, like plants, need the land to survive. One example of what happens when land is taken away is the character Muley, who has become a ghost of a man since his family went west, a dehumanized being who wanders, eats wild animals, and, nearly like a primitive man, lives in a cave. The banks have made him this way. Steinbeck believes that every inroad the banks take moves people one step farther from modern civilization. The Joads, like criminals, must hide from the deputies who patrol the land that until recently was theirs. Muley compares them to animals.

Grampa does not want to leave the land and needs to be sedated and hauled into the truck. He dies before they even make it out of Oklahoma. Pa also suffers greatly when they leave the land. Land to them is not merely soil, but their attachment to nature, to life itself. It is the adhesive that joins all living things into one. It is Ed Ricketts' philosophical legacy to John Steinbeck. Steinbeck felt that owning land endows one with responsibility to the community, the latter being a necessary component for his phalanx theory.

Chapter 11 (an interchapter) shows what happens when farmlands are abandoned. Vacated houses are no longer homes. While the tractors were plowing, there was some life, but once the engines are turned off, even the tractors are dead. However, the tractor driver never had the slightest idea of what the land really was or what he was doing to it.

The weather finds an easy victim and attacks the empty houses. It is followed by a phalanx of lower animals that invade the shards of buildings, survey the vacancy, and then leave. And when there is a little rain, weeds grow up in the doorway and between the floorboards.

Steinbeck's romantic belief that the farmer, attached to the soil, is shattered by the impersonal attack on the land by the tractor and the driver who has no understanding of how much damage he has done. And yet he counters that robotic creature by personifying the tractor as a being that goes home at the end of the day, and even dies. As in many of his other novels, Steinbeck

PERSONIFICATION—*A figure of speech in which an inanimate object is treated as, or compared to, a living thing.*

becomes distraught about people who do not understand each other or do not understand what harm they may be doing.

ROUTE 66

Chapter 12 is an interchapter on Route 66, the famed highway of American song and tale. The route goes directly from Mississippi to Bakersfield, California. It is the road of the migrants that crosses through myriad cities, through mountain ranges, over rivers, and into forests. And finally it reaches Bakersfield, and the migrants are overjoyed that they have reached their destination. But there is still need to fear. Will the jalopies make it through California, a large state? There is talk of a patrol at the California border to keep out all the workers who are coming in hordes. At its onset, this chapter seems to take on a biblical quality, almost like the story of the Israelites crossing the desert to the Promised Land.

"I" VERSUS "WE"

The western states are personified in Chapter 14, as if they are afraid of the coming of the migrants, government intervention, taxes, and labor unions. But what is coming is not the cause but the result. The cause, Steinbeck tells us, is hunger, which is caused by the banks that have thrown the farmers off their land. People, he claims, build, and as they do so, put themselves into what they build and then step away because they will grow bigger than their achievements. States are in for trouble when "I" becomes "we," because as individuals, people are vulnerable. As part of collectives, however, they are impenetrable.

This chapter is again impersonal; again by a pained narrator; again poetic. Those with power (financial and political) are frightened because angry farmworkers in large numbers are a threat. But it is their own fault; the powerful have created the hunger that drives these people to seek strength in banding together. People have the ability to achieve greatness and even then to improve on it. When they do not strive for improvement they are doomed. But this achievement is only accomplished when the individual becomes subordinate to the group. As long as the landowners deprive individuals of their human rights and force them to think only of themselves, the landowners win because they deter the farmworkers' formation of a union.

Some of the earlier questions are answered here. Steinbeck asks if the tractor is bad. His answer is no if the tractor belongs to "us," not "me"— on land that is "ours," not "mine." But as it is now, the tractor turns over the soil and turns away the farmer. It is possible that the threat of war in Europe is on his mind because his metaphors in this chapter are bombs and planes and tanks attacking individuals. But when an individual does not consider "I" there is hope. If the "I" in "I have lost my land" and "I have a little food" is replaced by "we" then the problem is the same but the feeling of loneliness and desperation is gone. Those who own are always the "I" and those who work for the owners are always the "we."

As much as this seems to make Steinbeck a Communist, he was not. He was a landowner himself, a product of free enterprise, a product of capitalism. He wrote books; he was paid well; he bought property with his money. What Steinbeck campaigned against were rich landowners who were becoming richer while the farm-workers were growing so poor that they were literally starving to death. Collectively, they could fight for a living wage and some health benefits. In unity there is strength.

THE NEW AMERICA

Rose of Sharon does not share the Joad's dream of a new life. She wants to be part of the America one sees in mag-azines—a home, a job, a baby. She cannot put faith in the hope of finding a nice piece of land to farm. Ma Joad reasserts her hold over the family by insisting they stay together. She began this journey with a premonition of disaster and cannot seem to lose it, but nevertheless will remain the family's center around which the others con-gregate. By now, however, the acceptance of the Wilsons as family, has made her domain even greater. She begins to encompass humankind as her family; she becomes the earth mother. Jim Casy plants the seed of doubt when he says that there are too many cars going in one direction. But the Joads continue.

OKIES

Cars cross the country like bugs, meandering about, ending up here and there. But in the evening, families camp next to each other and blend into each other as people meet and exchange ideas and opinions. These families become one family, much like the Joads and the Wilsons. And they all live by a set of rules that governs everything they do. Those who disobey are either ostracized or assaulted. Those who are wise and old become the leaders. The following morning, the society disbands and the individuals, like bugs, go their own way again.

The Okies, as they cross the country, create their own society each time they assemble at a campground. Without ever being written down, these rules are accepted by all the migrants because they are rules based on common sense, common values, and common concerns. The backbone of this society is equality, so that as each family bolsters the lives of the other families, the strength of "we" is felt by all. This society does not care about wealth or superiority and therefore does not develop leaders. Its wisdom comes from its elders. Once again, Steinbeck's style takes on a biblical tone, as if the rules have been set down by God for the Israelites crossing the desert.

THE DESERT

During the crossing of the desert, Granma dies but Ma will not tell anyone for fear it will keep them from their destination. By placing the Joads in the discomfort of the desert heat, Steinbeck is preparing the reader for the disappointments to follow, much as Moses had to cross the desert to come to his Promised Land. Again, as in the Bible, Steinbeck allows the Joads to see the beauty of the California greenery before them, as the Israelites saw it after the exodus.

CALIFORNIA'S HISTORY

In this interchapter, Steinbeck writes a brief, albeit biased, history of California, blaming the capitalists for chasing off the Mexicans and then putting foreign laborers into virtual slavery. He reiterates his theme of failure to understand. The migrants do not understand why the landowners let land lie fallow rather than permitting them to plant on it. They do not need to make a profit, they just need to grow enough to feed their families. The landowners cannot understand how the Okies could live the way they do, in shantytowns, crowded in tents, and under tarpaulins behind their trucks. They cannot understand why these poor, dirty people do not go home. When the camps grow too large, they too are destroyed because the authorities declare them a health and safety hazard. The landowners band together in a powerful association to keep the Okies from gaining too much power. They fear that 300,000 immigrants, all of whom are hungry and miserable, could overtake the landowners. Steinbeck believes that day will come.

ANGER

Steinbeck draws a thin line between hunger and anger. Whereas only the migrants feel hunger, anger is a key motivation for both sides of the battle. Local fruit pickers are angry that the migrants came to California in such great numbers. The more men available to work, the less money farmers will have to pay. Most accept the paltry wages because they were hungry. The landowners are angry because the migrants created an underclass that embarrassed them. The migrants are angry because the owners have them over a barrel: work for less, or do not work. A working class revolt is imminent.

Anger as a theme is explored further in Chapter 25. This interchapter describes how throughout California ripe grapes are not picked because the contractors cannot pay the wages of the men they need to pick the crop. The grapes become overripe and are made into bad wine. The entire state suffers. The scientific advancement of pesticides and grafting is useless if the crop is not harvested. Neither the rich nor the poor eat the fruit. The rotted fruit is burned, and the potatoes are dumped into the rivers. The children of the poor are plagued by disease, starving, and dying of malnutrition. The hungry are angry.

WEEDPATCH

The government camp of Weedpatch has toilets, showers, hot water and Saturday night dances. There are no police and the camp residents elect a committee to make the rules and to keep harmony in the camp. Rose of Sharon not only gets to take a bath but is informed that a resident nurse will help with the delivery of her child if she is still at Weedpatch.

Weedpatch is an example of what is reasonably close to a utopian society. Residents equally share all responsibilities. Officers are elected by a fair vote. People are treated with dignity. It may not be perfect, but it is a haven for the desperately poor migrants. It is the sanitary camp that Steinbeck visited while he was working on the *San Francisco News* articles, the place he toured with Tom Collins.

The Joads are turning back into the Joads they were before they left Oklahoma. The young men are working, the kids are playing, and Ma can tend to her motherly duties. Living in Weedpatch is also an educational experience. Winfield and Ruthie have never seen a flush toilet before. Some of the other residents need to be taught how to use some of the modern conveniences. But behind the dawning of this new world, trouble lurks. The banks, through the Farmers' Association, control the size of the salaries the contractors can pay. The Association will never allow the workers any say over their own lives and even concoct methods of intimidation to thwart the success of the government camps. The unity of the "we" has taken over the camp as everyone becomes equally involved in the upcoming dance.

Although Weedpatch is the highlight of the Joads' journey and comes the closest to a working manifestation of Steinbeck's phalanx theory, he himself was against the government having a greater role in peoples' lives than it already did. Establishments like Weedpatch should be temporary, just to help folks get back on their feet. "Nowhere in the novel does Steinbeck suggest that government should play a continuing role in shaping people's lives."[3]

THE FAMILY

Ma is the strongest character in the novel. She not only loses both her parents, but travels through the night next to her mother's corpse, keeping her death a secret so that the family does not stop in the desert. Ma does everything in her power to keep the family together. Nonetheless, throughout the journey, the family slowly disintegrates. First, the dog is killed on the highway; Grampa dies of a stroke before they leave Oklahoma; Granma dies before they reach California; Noah stays to live by the river; Rose of Sharon's husband runs off; Al decides to marry; and finally Tom decides to follow in Jim Casy's footsteps. Ma must give up the family unit she is trying so hard to maintain and give herself over to the concept of the bigger phalanx—the world.[4] This already began to happen when the Joads united with the Wilsons and then the Wainwrights, and when Ma left scraps of food for the starving kids although her own children were also hungry.

When Ma leaves Tom after he tells her he must go off, she does not cry, but suddenly it begins to rain, suggesting that if we are all part of one soul, the universal soul is doing the crying for Ma. Yet she is more able to handle the loss for she believes women can accept change better than men because they expect it. Men think they control their own destinies.

COTTON

Cotton pickers are needed. The pay is eighty cents a bag for the first pass through a field; ninety cents a bag for the second. Some pickers put rocks in the bottom of the bag so the bags are heavier. Some weighers fix the scales, so the bags show less than their actual weight. In time there will be more pickers than necessary. Steinbeck points out another way to defraud the laborers: offer them their cotton-picking bags on credit so they are in debt before they begin. Then rig the scales so they show less weight than is actually there. What can the pickers do? Check the scale before the bag is placed on it or drop a stone into the bag so they tip the scales in their favor? Corruption becomes a vicious cycle.

TOM THE DISCIPLE

Tom wants to follow in Casy's footsteps and organize strikes against the growers. Ma asks how she will know if Tom is safe or has been hurt. If Casy is right, he tells her, and we are all part of a larger soul, it will not matter if she and he are in contact because "I'll be everywhere— wherever you look. Whenever they's a fight so hungry people can eat, I'll be there. Wherever they's a cop beatin' up a guy, I'll be there. . . . An' when our folks eat the stuff they raise an' live in the house they build—why I'll be there." He is becoming part of the transcendental over-soul. Tom says goodbye to his mother in a womb-like cave. When he emerges, he will be symbolically reborn.

Just as Steinbeck presented Casy as Christ, he now presents Tom as Casy's disciple. Tom accepts Casy's belief that we are all part of one soul. And if it is true, then whenever people assemble to defend their rights, his spirit will always be within those men. And when people attain the dignity of leading their own lives, his spirit will be part of it. He vows that he will continue Casy's campaign for justice for the oppressed migrant workers.

THE WATERS

In the last interchapter Steinbeck talks about the devastation caused by heavy rains. Rivers overflow and trees come tumbling down. Fields become lakes. Cars are abandoned because they no longer are able to start. The migrant tent camps become unlivable places. Finally, the worst consequences: no work, no income. Steinbeck's style reverts once again to biblical cadences.

The Joads are now living on the Hooper ranch in half of one of twelve boxcars whose wheels have been removed. The Wainwrights occupy the other half. This echoes the way they lived in Oklahoma—half-a-house per family. This also brings back the turtle, who lives in a half-shell.

Nature, at its most powerful, is responsible for the Joads being captured. They cannot leave because the river is overflowing and because Rose of Sharon has gone into labor. The water, symbol of life and motherhood, is raging out of control. The only possible means of curbing the flooding river is through a group effort. At first, the men only think of themselves, but Mr. Wainwright's plea influences them so they now begin to think as "we" and create a phalanx to fight the river by building an embankment.

In the midst of the rain, Rose of Sharon gives birth to a stillborn child. Uncle John places the baby in an apple box and floats it in the stream, saying: "Go down an' tell 'em." Uncle John reenacts the incident in the Bible of the baby Moses being placed into the river that will carry him to safety. Alas, this Moses—who could have led the people to the Promised Land—is dead.

Steinbeck ends the novel with a sentimental moment that gently hints at a bit of hope. Rose of Sharon, whose life has been one of misery and disappointment, saves the life of a stranger by offering him her breast milk. This is another reference out of the Bible: "I [Christ] am the rose of Sharon, and the lily of the valleys" (Canticles 2:1).[5] And Rose of Sharon offers up her body as Christ does his. The man suckles and a smile comes across Rose of Sharon's face, just as it did across Jim Casy's face when he sacrificed himself to be arrested instead of Tom.

The Joads have learned that they are more than just a

single family but are members of a larger entity. They are what Casy had hoped all humanity would be. Steinbeck presents the idea that enlightenment is attained only once we have overcome being self-absorbed and we widen our devotion to the world at large, a family of which we are all a part. [6]

COPING
WITH FAME

After *The Grapes of Wrath* was published, John Steinbeck was deluged with mail. People he hardly knew were coming out of the woodwork to ask him for a handout. They were stopping by his ranch in Monterey as if they were long-lost friends. Being a private person, he was unhappy with becoming public property. He was criticized for his Communist leanings, as they were apparent to some, in *The Grapes of Wrath*. The book was banned in several cities for its obscenity. However, it continued to be the number-one best-seller for the entire year.

Eleanor Roosevelt, the President's wife, repeatedly defended Steinbeck's portrayal of the Okies and work camps. Steinbeck was so grateful he wrote to her in thanks. He said he was being called a liar so often he was beginning to question his own personal accounts of what happened. The film releases of *The Grapes of Wrath* and *Of Mice and Men* increased public support for Steinbeck, as the films could translate for the general public the actual dimension of the suffering the characters felt. Steinbeck was awarded the Pulitzer Prize for Literature for *The Grapes of Wrath*.

One day John Steinbeck received a phone call from Hollywood. He was offered $5,000 a week to write movie scripts. Carol immediately got on the phone and said, "What the hell would we do with $5,000 a week?" and hung up.[1] Steinbeck had finally achieved financial freedom.

GWYN

Meanwhile, John and Carol were drifting apart. In June 1940, Steinbeck returned to Hollywood despite Carol's objections. He took a small apartment near his friend Max Wagner. One evening, Max took Steinbeck to a small nightclub to hear his friend Gwendolyn Conger sing. Steinbeck was very taken by her. Gwen (or Gwyn—she changed her name in 1941) was twenty, and Steinbeck was thirty-eight. But he was not yet ready to give up on his marriage to Carol.

Steinbeck decided to go on a sea expedition with Ed Ricketts both to satisfy his yearning for science and to get some space from Carol, but she insisted on coming along. John wanted to write a log, or diary, on what he experienced. A large fishing boat was hired for the expedition, whose goal was to find out as much as possible about the marine life off the coast of California and Mexico. Steinbeck's observation of the Mexican people and how they lived compared to Americans made him realize

Mexicans were happy to be Mexicans. Only Americans thought Mexicans were poor, unhappy people, because they were judging them by American standards. The expedition down to the Sea of Cortez lasted about a month, and Steinbeck's *The Log of the Sea of Cortez* was published in 1941.

Back home, Steinbeck thought about using the humor of *Tortilla Flat* to tell the stories of the people and countryside of Monterey, and he began collecting tales for *Cannery Row*. He also began writing *Forgotten Village*, a film in which a poor Mexican family gets caught up in politics and religion. Lewis Milestone, the producer of *Of Mice and Men*, wanted to follow up his huge success with a film of *The Red Pony*. The New York City Board of Censors rejected *The Forgotten Village*. They felt the movie was "indecent," because of the lack of clothing worn by the Mexican peasants. They also felt the film "promoted socialism." Steinbeck's good friend, First Lady Eleanor Roosevelt, intervened, and the ban against *The Forgotten Village* was lifted.

When they finally got back to Los Gatos, John could see his relationship with Carol had not improved. Steinbeck suspected that Carol was jealous of him and his achievements.[2] So he often escaped to San Francisco to visit Gwyn. It seemed as if Steinbeck did not care if people saw him with another woman.

Carol confronted John about his affair with Gwyn in March and left him for good by April. Steinbeck occupied his time by working on *The Sea of Cortez* with Ed Ricketts.

He would stay at the apartment above the lab. He sent the completed manuscript to Viking at the end of July. During this period of time, Carol moved to New York. John and Gwyn moved to the Pacific Grove house, and later, to New York City. At the age of forty, Steinbeck wanted to settle down and have children.[3]

By mid-October, Steinbeck received an invitation from President Roosevelt to be part of a committee that would find ways to combat the Nazi propaganda machine. Other writers included Thornton Wilder, Stephen Vincent Benet, and Robert Sherwood, also a Pulitzer Prize-winning playwright. This committee was set up under the auspices of the Foreign Information Service. Steinbeck's role was to meet many refugees who had escaped their occupied countries. They had stories to tell him about the resistance, and how these small secret armies pledged to fend off the Germans in any way they could. This information formed the basis for his next project, *The Moon is Down*. He began writing it as a play, much as he did when he was writing *Of Mice and Men*.

THE MOON IS DOWN

Steinbeck offered his manuscript of *The Moon Is Down* to the FIS. They rejected it because it depicted a foreign occupation on American soil. They felt it would demoralize Americans if even a hint of foreign occupation was mentioned. Steinbeck rewrote the manuscript with the action taking place overseas. In March, *The Moon Is Down* was

ready to be published. Steinbeck was working with Oscar
Serlin, a Broadway producer, to turn it into a Broadway
play. When the play was produced, it ran for nine weeks
on Broadway, and was hugely successful overseas. The
Book of the Month Club had ordered 200,000 copies in
advance, which topped the advance order for *The Grapes of
Wrath*. However, the general critical consensus was that
The Moon Is Down was a piece of outright propaganda, with
characters who had no dimension to them. A *New York
Times* reviewer called it "the most memorable fiction to
come out of the war," whereas other critics, such as
Clifton Fadiman and James Thurber, attacked it as "fairy
tale in nature."[4] It was, nonetheless, a perfect propaganda
vehicle. It appeared in seventy-six editions, between 1945
and 1989, and was translated into many languages
including Korean, Urdu, Slovak, and Burmese. *The Moon Is
Down* sold more than a million copies before the year
ended. His earnings were almost quadrupled compared to
what he earned for *The Grapes of Wrath*. For the most part,
Steinbeck could not believe how much money he was
making from a book that was not his best writing.

At this time, Carol Steinbeck was making strong
demands for a divorce settlement. She felt she should
have a portion of the material benefits Steinbeck was
enjoying, since she had been very supportive of him during his early writing career. A very generous settlement
was worked out. John and Gwyn moved across the
Hudson River to a house in Sneden's Landing, a town
popular with movie stars and other famous people who

wanted their privacy. While there, Steinbeck still worked with the FIS, writing broadcasts he would send to Washington, D.C., for possible airing.

Steinbeck was asked to write a book about the training of bomber crews, which eventually became *Bombs Away: The Story of a Bomber Team*. The book enjoyed strong sales and its film rights were sold for $250,000. Steinbeck donated the money to the Air Force Aid Society Trust Fund. Many critics believed this was one of Steinbeck's best pieces of journalism and the bomber crew experience exemplified his phalanx theory.

In September, John and Gwyn moved to Sherman Oaks, California, where John was to work on the film version of *The Moon Is Down*. He also coauthored the script of a film called *A Medal for Benny*. The film was released in 1945, and largely forgotten. One of his films that had received more attention was *Lifeboat*. It was a story about how the victims of a U-boat sinking tried to survive on a lifeboat. Again, it demonstrated the phalanx theory as all the members in the boat had to work together to save themselves. Twentieth-Century Fox approved the script, and Alfred Hitchcock, the British director who would become famous as the master of suspense films, was asked to direct. *Lifeboat* was released in January 1943 and made Steinbeck furious. The script he had delivered had not been followed to the letter. Someone had changed the black character into a stock comic, a simple role. Steinbeck did not have that in mind. There were also slurs made against organized labor, something Steinbeck would never do. He laid most of the blame on the director's doorstep. Hitchcock was a man he considered "one of those incredible middle-class English snobs."[5] Steinbeck vowed he would never again work with people he did not know and could not trust.

John and Gwyn married on March 29, 1943, and moved back to New York to East Fifty-Eighth Street. They settled into the bottom half of a townhouse, which had all the touches of home, including a fireplace and a garden, which Steinbeck especially liked.

WAR CORRESPONDENT

For many months, Steinbeck had expressed interest in becoming a war correspondent for the *New York Herald Tribune*. But getting approval from the War Department was difficult. Some people who were interviewed about Steinbeck and his patriotism had made negative comments. They had not forgotten *The Grapes of Wrath* and continued their condemnation of him as a Communist and a radical. He finally received clearance from the War Department and immediately shipped out, leaving his new wife behind. Steinbeck was in the European Theatre of Operations for five months. His dispatches were popular and widely read all over the world. In August, Steinbeck received permission to go to North Africa. He attached himself to a special operations unit where he was able to watch the invasion of Italy by the Allied troops. It was Steinbeck's first contact with the blood and guts of real battle, and some say it had a lifelong effect upon him. The experience had left him with a ruptured eardrum, sporadic memory loss, and serious depression. His dispatches from the war were collected in the book *Once There Was a War*, which was published in 1958.

CANNERY ROW AND THE PEARL

On October 15, 1943, Steinbeck returned home to Gwyn and began working on *Cannery Row*, to cheer himself up. This was a bright, cheerful book with many unusual and funny characters. In March, Steinbeck worked with Lewis Milestone to put together a film package for *The Pearl*. *The Pearl* is a mythical story of a Mexican Indian pearl diver named Kino. When he finds a valuable pearl, the greedy townsfolk try to steal it or otherwise cheat him. Something that he was hoping would save his poverty-stricken family, instead inspires greed, vice, and finally, death. Concluding that the pearl is cursed, Kino throws it back into the ocean. Kino's tragedy is thereafter told as a legend in the town.

On August 2, 1944, Thom Steinbeck was born. John Steinbeck finished *Cannery Row*, which would come out in January, and was in the middle of writing *The Pearl*. But he hinted to Dook Sheffield that in the back of his mind he was contemplating another "Big Book."

John, Gwyn, and Thom returned to Monterey and purchased the Soto House, a well-known landmark, built in 1830. John was glad to be back with Ed Ricketts, who was the basis for *Cannery Row*'s main character, Doc. *Cannery Row* is a comical story of the denizens of the poor but colorful area of Monterey that is full of sardine canneries and whorehouses.

When *Cannery Row* came out, in January 1945, there were many negative reviews. One critic called it a "poisoned creampuff of American life." Another said it showed that Steinbeck had "coasted" on the tails of *The Grapes of Wrath*, calling the story of a bunch of bums and prostitutes planning a party for the retiring "Doc" of *Cannery Row* inconsequential and pompous at the same time. Nonetheless, the sales of *Cannery Row* were tremendous and the film rights were sold. The citizens of Monterey, however, felt *Cannery Row* was an insult to their town and began giving the Steinbecks the cold shoulder.

Meanwhile, Steinbeck went back to completing his first draft of *The Pearl*. On February 14, he left for Mexico to begin polishing it. Gwyn joined John and traveled all over Mexico, listening to traditional Mexican music, so she could write the score for the film version.

During the summer of 1945, a film company approached Steinbeck to write a script about the Mexican revolutionary Emiliano Zapata, but Steinbeck insisted the film company get permission from the Mexican government. Steinbeck had not been pleased the way *Forgotten Village* had been completed in Mexico and he did not want to go through that again.

BACK IN NEW YORK

Upon his return to New York, John bought two adjacent brownstones on East Eighty-Fifth Street in Manhattan. Gwyn became pregnant with their second child and felt thoroughly neglected, as John went off to Mexico to begin filming *The Pearl*. John Steinbeck IV was born on June 12, 1946. Gwyn stayed in her bed while nannies and nurses took care of Thom and the baby. Although Steinbeck was happy about the birth of his second son, he felt that what went on at home upstairs from his basement workroom was not his business. Friends began to notice the rift between John and Gwyn. While they both liked the social whirl, John actually may have been going out more frequently to avoid confronting Gwyn and her problems. The age difference was crucial. According to some, Gwyn was acting like a spoiled, demanding brat. She was still carrying a grudge against John for leaving her at very important times in her life and for supposedly ruining her singing career.

John was writing *The Wayward Bus* in his basement hideout. He also took a trip to Mexico to see the completion of the filming of *The Pearl*. Once Steinbeck completed *The Wayward Bus*, he accepted an invitation from his Danish publisher to visit Denmark, where he was extremely popular. Apparently, *The Moon Is Down* helped keep up the morale of the people who were involved in the Danish resistance. The Danish king invited Steinbeck to the palace and bestowed upon him the Liberty Cross, one of the highest honors awarded to an American by

Denmark. Gwyn felt dwarfed by her husband's success. Back in New York, John and Gwyn sometimes went on for days without speaking to each other. They still went out socially and the lack of closeness between them became more obvious to their friends. Gwyn also began an affair with a man several years her junior.

The Wayward Bus was published in February, just before Steinbeck's birthday. The critics were not kind. In the novel, the bus travels on a little used route in California, and picks up people from all walks of life. Steinbeck was supposedly trying to use the bus as a metaphor for the United States as a "melting pot." Some critics called the book overly sexy. Frank O'Malley, a critic for Commonwealth magazine, said The Wayward Bus "has no real human or universal significance. It is nothing more than an unusually dismal bus ride."[6] Steinbeck later admitted that the novel had been "a paste-up job."[7] A total of 750,000 copies were sold through a combination of The Book of the Month Club, and Viking's own printing. The Wayward Bus was one of Steinbeck's most successful books.

RUSSIA

Steinbeck needed something to occupy his time so he would not have to think about his unhappy life with Gwyn. He took the Herald Tribune up on a suggestion to report from Europe, now that the war was over. One night, he saw Robert Capa, a photographer and friend he originally met during the war. Capa suggested they go to Russia and create a journal-like book on the average Russian, about whom Americans knew very little.

Capa and Steinbeck flew to Moscow, and they immediately had trouble with their hotel reservations. It took almost a week to get permission to travel to the Ukraine and Georgia. The Cold War had begun and suddenly everything between Americans and Russians was treated with suspicion. Capa could not even develop pictures he had taken until he was issued a permit. All the Americans' moves were closely watched by Intourist, the Russian tourist organization. Eventually, all of Steinbeck's observations would be published as *The Russian Journal*. He was criticized by some for his unsophisticated view of the Russian versus the American political agenda. But, his depictions of the Russian people and the countryside were well received. Steinbeck concluded, "Russian people are like all other people in the world. Some bad ones there are, but, by far, the greater number are very good."[8]

Steinbeck was ready for something big. Upon his return to New York, he wrote to his friend and fellow writer John O'Hara, "I've been practicing for a book for thirty-five years and this is it."[9] He mentioned this idea to Gwyn, and explained that it would be fitting if they moved back to California as he proceeded with his "great work." She would not hear of it. To John, this signified the end of the marriage.

While Steinbeck was in Russia both the book and the film *The Pearl* were released. Most critics thought the story was simplistic, and the book sales were not considerable. It would take a number of years before *The Pearl* would be considered a classic.

THE DEATH OF ED RICKETTS

Although, Steinbeck's writing was often ridiculed by book critics, in the film industry he was well respected. In 1948, he had two movies in various stages of production, *The Red Pony* and *Cannery Row*. In addition, Steinbeck became a partner in a company that would package television shows. While many talented people in the film industry were eager to sign on with the new company, it did not amount to much. But it was a nice dream to contemplate for Steinbeck. John also found time to renew his friendship with Ed Ricketts. The two made plans for an expedition to British Columbia.

John had to return to New York where he was scheduled to have surgery on his legs for the removal of varicose veins. He recovered at the Bedford Hotel, alone. In the first week of May, Steinbeck was notified that Ed Ricketts had been in a terrible automobile accident and was not expected to live. Steinbeck immediately flew back to the West Coast. But it was too late for him to say goodbye. Steinbeck returned to the lab and burned all of Ricketts personal correspondence to him. Steinbeck felt he had lost "the greatest man I have ever known and the best teacher."[10] For Steinbeck, physically weakened by his surgery, without a book to keep him focused, and uncertain about the future of his marriage and children, the loss of Ed Ricketts was a serious blow.

In the midst of all this, Steinbeck would set out to write his most ambitious writing project.

THE LAST
BIG BOOK

Upon returning to New York, Steinbeck took a suite at the Bedford Hotel. Gwyn told him she wanted a divorce. She moved with the boys to California and was planning to demand a huge settlement. Steinbeck was alone and miserable. Elia Kazan came to the rescue and offered Steinbeck the opportunity to write the screenplay for *Viva Zapata*.

Steinbeck flew to Cuernavaca and dove into his work. He traveled through Mexico, doing research on Emiliano Zapata. In September, Steinbeck returned to his Pacific Grove house. He did not write. Friends who visited him worried about his mental state.

In November, he and Elia Kazan, who would direct *Viva Zapata*, went to Cuernavaca. Kazan was upset about Steinbeck's condition, both physically and mentally. No matter what the two of them did, Steinbeck could not shake his depression. He returned to Pacific Grove in late November, desperately wanting to capture the happy remnants of his childhood. Happily, he learned that he would have custody of his two boys for the following summer.

Another ray of sunshine for Steinbeck was the news that he had been elected to the American Academy of Arts and Letters, along with William Faulkner, Mark Van Doren, and Leon Kroll.

Steinbeck wrote feverishly through the winter and early spring to complete *Viva Zapata*. One day in April, Steinbeck felt the need to see his sons. He flew back to New York and stayed for a week at the Bedford Hotel, so he was able to see them everyday.

ELAINE

Upon his return to Hollywood, Steinbeck became more social and even began dating the likes of actress Ann Sothern. She introduced him to her friend, Elaine Scott, who had been a stage manager in New York. Elaine was from Texas—bright, funny, and knew a lot of Hollywood and Broadway people. Elaine was in the process of divorcing the actor Zachary Scott. John and Elaine began dating but kept it a secret from all but Steinbeck's closest friends.

When Steinbeck was finishing his draft of *Viva Zapata* and beginning his notes on another book, Thom and John IV came for their mid-summer visit, something Steinbeck was eagerly awaiting. Elaine Scott drove up to meet them and join in the "family" fun. Steinbeck was truly happy. He really did have a home again. And, as it turned out, he was able to keep the boys well into September because of an outbreak of polio in New York.

Steinbeck thought about another idea for a play or a

novel, which would eventually become *Burning Bright,* as he continued to work on the script for *Viva Zapata* with Elia Kazan. He also wrote an introduction to the new edition of *The Sea of Cortez,* under the title of *The Log from The Sea of Cortez.*

The summer of 1950 Steinbeck rented a farmhouse in Rockland County, New York, and had everyone there: the boys, Elaine and her daughter, Waverly, and the boys' tutor. He was preparing for the play version of *Burning Bright,* which was scheduled to go into rehearsal at the beginning of September. The play itself was written as a morality tale and he feared it would be "over the heads" of a regular Broadway audience. And so it was. The play opened to bad reviews all around.

The wedding of Elaine Scott and John Steinbeck took place on December 28. John bought a brownstone on East 72nd Street, in which they would live for the next thirteen years.

SALINAS VALLEY, THE NOVEL

After his honeymoon, John Steinbeck began writing *Salinas Valley* (later, *East of Eden*). He knew this was going to be another big one—"what I have been practicing to write all my life."[1] Steinbeck envisioned the book as a family history for Thom and John IV. Although he knew it would take the form of a novel, he kept a journal too where he could record his reactions while writing the novel. It is in this journal that Steinbeck dedicates the book to his children. The journal was later published as *Journal of a Novel: The "East of Eden" Letters*. In this journal, Steinbeck writes that he plans to tell the boys the greatest story of all, "the story of good and evil, strength and weakness, of love and hate, of beauty and ugliness," and "shall demonstrate to them how these doubles are inseparable, how neither can exist without the other, and how, out of their groupings, creativeness is born."[2]

When the boys would come to visit, they were left in Elaine's care. The boys, who resented the absence of their father, did their utmost to act out.[3] In the early part of June, Steinbeck changed the title of his "big book" from *Salinas Valley* to *East of Eden*, as he became more fascinated with the Cain and Abel story in the Bible. He was able to weave this story through both the Hamilton and Trask families. Steinbeck, who was always careful to do complete research on anything he wrote, found an alternative meaning for the Hebrew word *tlmshel*, which was very important to the end at East of Eden. For Steinbeck's purposes, the word no longer meant "thou shalt not," it meant "thou mayest," and therefore gave man greater responsibility for his own actions. When Adam Trask, the father of Cal, is on his deathbed, he is asked to forgive Cal for the death of his brother Aaron. He utters the word *timshel*, freeing Cal to live without the weight of a guilty conscience and follow a new path.

Steinbeck used three hundred pencils and thirty reams of paper for this project. The original manuscript of the novel ran to 350,000 words and the journal, 75,000 words.[4] The finished manuscript was delivered to Pat Covici in a hand-carved wooden box created by Steinbeck.

HUAC

By February 1952, the revisions were finished on *East of Eden*, and Steinbeck decided he and Elaine should go abroad. Steinbeck would write articles for *Collier's* magazine. While in Spain, Steinbeck learned that his good friend, filmmaker Elia Kazan, had testified before the House Un-American Activities Committee (HUAC). Most people in Hollywood would not appear before this congressional committee because they refused to testify against their fellow artists and name names of alleged Communist sympathizers. This was one of the darkest times in American history. As the committee's power increased, it began to seem like a "witch hunt." Those who were perceived to be "left-leaning" in the film industry were "blacklisted," unable to work in Hollywood. Those who did testify were considered traitors to the cause of artistic freedom.

Steinbeck defended Kazan. He called Kazan "a good and honest man," and hoped "the Communists would not cut Kazan to pieces."[5] This was a surprise to many. They had expected Steinbeck, with his extensive knowledge of the plight of the downtrodden exemplified in *The Grapes of Wrath* and *In Dubious Battle*, to sympathize with the platform of the Communist party. But his friendship with

Kazan, especially after the death of Ed Ricketts, was of such importance to Steinbeck that he had to support him. On the other hand, he would heartily defend the right of Lillian Hellman, an American novelist and playwright, not to testify before the Committee. Steinbeck was a patriot, but he was also a friend and an honest American.

EAST OF EDEN

E ast of Eden is the story of three generations of two families, the Trasks and the Hamiltons, from the mid-1800s to World War I. Both families move from the eastern U. S. to California in hope of finding fertile lands and sunshine. *East of Eden*, in four books and fifty-five chapters, is based on people with whom Steinbeck was familiar. His motivation for writing this saga was to create an enduring legacy for his two sons, Thom and John IV, whom he loved very much. The characters in the Hamilton family were based upon Steinbeck's maternal grandparents. There really was a Samuel Hamilton, and the character of Olive is based on Steinbeck's mother.

Within this family saga, many themes are evident. Among them are the bible stories of Cain and Abel, Adam and Eve, and the Garden of Eden. Other themes include the nature of good and evil, saving the environment, the group versus the individual, a child's vulnerability to the actions of his parents before him, and a child's fear that his parents do not love him.

The plot weaves from the Hamiltons to the Trasks,

from one chapter to another. Certain critics felt that Steinbeck set out to write the history of the Hamiltons but then got overly interested in the Trasks and would have been better off just sticking to one family. The voice of the author appears as commentary or as character, which critics and readers have found confusing, especially when the narrator uses the "I" and "we" pronouns. There is even a point where the real John Steinbeck, as a child, comes in contact with the fictional Adam Trask.

To John Steinbeck, *East of Eden* was his most meaningful and heartfelt work.

CAIN AND ABEL

The Cain and Abel biblical allegory, which begins through the characters Adam and Charles, is one of fraternal innocence and envy. Abel is the favored child of Adam and Eve. He is the fair-haired boy, so to speak. He is a herdsman, while Cain tends the land. Cain cannot win his father's love, no matter what he does. Cain's jealousy gets the better of him, and he kills Abel. He tries to hide this misdeed from his father, and when asked where Abel is, he implies he does not know. "Am I my brother's keeper?" he asks. Because he has killed his brother, Cain is expelled from the Garden of Eden. God affords him protection, however, by putting a mark on his forehead, which will prevent him from being killed. Cain is later credited with founding the first city.

Some critics have found the allegory as presented in

the novel too didactic, or too obvious. For example, all the main characters that typify evil in the eyes of Steinbeck have names that begin with the letter "C" (Cyrus, Charles, Cathy, Caleb). In addition, Charles and Cathy both have big scars on their foreheads. The names of all the good characters begin with the letter "A" (Alice, Adam, Aron, Abra). Yet their names are about the only thing that is obvious. The Cain and Abel parallels in *East of Eden* are not straightforward at all; instead they weave from brother to brother, sometimes inverting themselves, making the "Abel" character evil, and making the "Cain" character good. The conclusion Steinbeck wants the reader to draw is that every person has both good and evil within and must learn to reconcile the two.

The first Cain character is Cyrus. His first Abel counterpart is Adam's mother, who commits suicide because of Cyrus' infidelity. The second "Abel" is Alice, Cain's mother. The wives are meek and good, while Cyrus is lying, cheating, and tyrannical. Being the first father in the novel, he is also an Adam-like character, the first man, father to Cain and Abel in the Bible. Yet, rather than Eve leading to his fall, it is he who brings sin and poison to his wives (in the form of a venereal disease). Since he is also the father of the novel's Adam, he could be seen as a God-like character, or, more accurately, a Satan-like character. He is even described as "something of a devil."[1]

Cyrus' sons, Adam and Charles, are the Abel and Cain brothers. In the Bible, Cain is the first-born and, therefore, his jealousy is somewhat justified because the first son traditionally received the family inheritance and the father's favor. In the case of Adam and Charles, however, Adam is born first and so the sibling order is not disrupted when Cyrus prefers him. Unlike the Biblical story, Adam actually wants to win his stepmother's affection. He resents Cyrus' attention, and later confesses that he always hated him. There is no clear reason why Cyrus prefers Adam to Charles, other than his being first-born. The two details that follow the Biblical story are that Cyrus prefers Adam's gift of the puppy over Charles' gift of the pocketknife and that Charles attacks Adam, although he does not actually kill him. After the attack, however, it is Charles who settles down on the farm and Adam who is exiled into the army and thereafter wanders the land.

Adam's twin sons, Caleb and Aron, are the second pair of Cain and Abel brothers.

Sam says: "Names are a great mystery. I've never known whether the name is molded by the child changed to fit the name."[2] Perhaps that is why they are named after Biblical characters Caleb and Aron, which are the reverse of Cain and Abel. In the Bible Caleb was the only one of his generation (together with Joshua) allowed into the land of Canaan, whereas Aron betrayed Moses by making a golden calf for the Jews to worship. It is as if the symbolisms of the different parts of the name are meant to balance out: the C in Caleb is evil, whereas the Biblical meaning of Caleb is virtuous; the A of Aron is virtuous, but the Biblical Aron is far from good.

111

Aron Trask is fair and well-liked, yet physically he resembles his evil mother, Cathy. In fact, that is why Adam prefers him to his brother, Caleb, because he reminds him of Cathy. Adam seems as arbitrary as Cyrus in his preference of one son over the other. If anything, Adam should dislike the son who looks like Cathy, at least after her curse on him is lifted. But even after Adam is free of Cathy, he continues to reject Caleb in favor of Aron. Although Adam realizes how a father's preference of a sibling can lead to rivalry, he repeats Cyrus' detrimental behavior.

Steinbeck illustrates the difference between Caleb and Aron using an anthill. Aron would observe the anthill, while Cal (as Caleb is called) would knock it down and kill all the ants. Cal is always seething with anger over the rejection he feels because everyone favors Aron. Aron raises rabbits and Caleb tends to the garden, in accordance with the Biblical allegory. Both strive for their father's love and also for schoolmate Abra's love. Abra falls for Aron, thereby rejecting Caleb. But Caleb's cunning leads her to reject Aron's gift of a rabbit. Yet later, Abra, a wholly positive character, falls out of love with Aron because she senses a religious hypocrisy about him. For one thing, Aron becomes too close to Mr. Rolf, the self-righteous minister. He also asks Abra to be celibate with him and begins to construct a false reality around himself when he is unable to reconcile the good and evil in his nature.

Caleb earns $15,000 by speculating on beans and

presents it to his father to make up for the loss he incurred through his failed lettuce venture. Caleb is entrepreneurial, just like Cain was after his crime. His father rejects the money and tells Cal he wishes he led a life like Aron's. Caleb becomes so angry with his father's rejection that he decides to take it out on Aron. He leads Aron to the whorehouse and introduces him to their real mother. Aron is so overwhelmed by this, he enlists in the army and is later killed. So Caleb indirectly kills Aron, just like Cain killed Abel.

In a twist on the Biblical allegory, Adam is persuaded to forgive Caleb his transgressions. He utters the Hebrew word *timshel*, thereby giving his son the freedom to change his fate. Caleb is then able to reconcile the good and the evil within him, which Aron could not do. Because of his abilities to face reality and also to be an entrepreneurial success, "Cal is not only the universal Everyman in the novel, but also the representative American figure."[3]

CATHY

Many critics thought the character of Cathy Ames was based, in part, on Steinbeck's second wife, Gwyn. The "Moral Monster," according to Steinbeck, is introduced in the Cathy Ames character. She hides her evil ways under a heart-shaped face of innocence. She is a liar who knows how to manipulate the truth. She learned very early that sexuality is useful. To Steinbeck, Cathy was evil incarnate.

There is no rational reason for her behavior. She is just something that happened. Many critics felt that the character of Cathy weakens the novel because she is so inhuman.

In the 1950s, when *East of Eden* was published, the character of Cathy was sensational. The emphasis on her blatant sexual nature was very daring. In addition, a mother not wanting her own babies was unheard of.

The idea that Adam would fall in love with Cathy immediately and Charles would see right through her, points to Adam's assumptions about the goodness of all people and Charles' more realistic assessment of himself and others. He still sees himself as the child who was never loved by his father. The idea that we may not be in charge of our own fate and may be subject to the randomness of nature and events was a philosophy constantly on Steinbeck's mind. He desperately wanted his own sons to find their own way and be successful in life despite having a troubled mother and a father who found it difficult to express his deep love for his children.

One of the reasons Cathy (or Kate as she is known at the whorehouse) commits suicide is because she no longer has a terrifying affect on people like Adam and Caleb. Caleb tells her his wickedness is his own, not hers. Cal is clearly different from his mother because he has a conscience; he is constantly conflicted over hurting Aron. He loves Adam and Aron. Cathy, on the other hand, never loved anyone and only rejoiced in her evil deeds.

When she dies, Cathy leaves all her money to Aron,

possibly in one last attempt to destroy him.[4] Gifts of money do not lead to good things in *East of Eden*. Caleb's $15,000 led to rejection, anger, murder, and guilt. In fact, he had to burn the money. A generation prior to that, Cyrus left his sons a fortune that he had accrued by cheating. Adam convinced Charles to accept their inheritance because they never before received what they needed from their father (love, in particular). Furthermore, both Cyrus' and Cathy's money were earned through corrupt deeds. Caleb's $15,000 was earned through speculation, which Adam did not condone. Perhaps the theme of wealth as corruption is indicative of Steinbeck's fear that money would be the only thing his sons would take away from him.

LEE

Lee is Adam Trask's servant. Many critics felt he is far too convenient and wise to be a real human being.[5] Lee, like Sam Hamilton, is there to help Adam and his sons with good advice. Some critics believe the character of Lee was based upon Joe Higashi, the Japanese houseboy, whom the Steinbecks hired at their Los Gatos ranch.

In Chapter 15, Sam and Lee have a philosophical conversation in which Steinbeck speaks his message on racism in America through both characters. Sam asks Lee why he speaks "pidgin," when he is able to speak perfect English. Lee tells Sam that is what people expect from a Chinese man. Lee and Sam talk about stereotyping. Sam asks why Lee still wears a long braid, (or queue) if he is no longer a slave to the Mandarin Chinese. Lee explains it would not make a difference. People still will see him as Chinese no matter what he did. In Lee's case, his physical appearance prevents him from "fitting in." Lee also tells Sam that he tried going to China, but the Chinese people considered him a foreigner as well. Lee tells Sam he is a servant because ". . . a good servant is the refuge of the philosopher . . . a good servant can completely control his master."[6]

Ironically enough, Lee discloses the true meaning of the Hebrew word *timshel* to Adam. Lee had to go to Chinese philosophers to learn this meaning. Therefore, Lee is the truest proponent of free will in the novel. He firmly believes that children do not have to repeat their parents' mistakes. Lee also retells the story of Cain and Abel with an added emphasis on the role rejection plays in the course of events. He suggests that rejection led to anger, murder, and guilt. Lee concludes that this is the story of every man, since he believes all of mankind originated with Cain. Lee notes that all men repeat the mistake of rejecting their children, which leads to anger and worse.

Lee is the voice of reason throughout the novel. He helps save Caleb from ruin. Lee discloses to Cal that his mother committed suicide. He talks about two opposites in human beings (weak/strong and cruel/kind). Lee tries to convince Cal he is not all evil, even if he did make Aron run away. Abra argues the same point with Cal. She is like an extension of Lee, who even said he wishes she were his daughter. Abra maintains that the reason Aron ran away is because he could not deal with the truth about his mother. According to Abra, Aron created a story of a world he wanted to live in and the truth about Cathy did not fit into his story. Aron was unable to deal with reality. Abra tells Cal that the reason she likes him is that he does not live in a story.

Lee tells Adam it was because of his rejection that Cal inadvertantly caused the death of Aron. Lee persuades Adam to help his only living son by giving him a chance to live without this rejection. He asks Adam to bless him. Adam says "timshel," thereby granting Cal the "free will" to overcome his guilt and go on with his life.

TIMSHEL

Lee talks about the time he was studying the Bible and had to consult the original Hebrew version. He wanted to know the meaning of the Hebrew word *timshel*, which God utters to Cain in relation to overcoming sin. Lee was confused as to whether that word meant "thou shalt," or "do thou." With the help of the Chinese philosophers, he was able to reach the conclusion that the word meant "thou mayest," meaning God did not command Cain to triumph over sin; rather, he suggested that Cain may overcome sin if he chooses to. This indicates that man does indeed have free will and is not always bound by what has happened before. He mentions that he has never been so proud of his own people for having discovered this. It has restored Lee's faith in the human soul, because he can make his own choice.

Steinbeck's doctrine of free will is similar to Milton's in *Paradise Lost*, which is a story of Adam and Eve and their fall from grace. "Milton's epic is an attempt to justify the ways of God to man. Steinbeck is more interested in justifying the ways of men to men and of each individual to himself."[7]

Interestingly enough, the concept of *timshel* does not apply to Cathy, Aron, or Adam (for the most part). Only Caleb can change what he deems to be his fate. Cathy, on the other hand, was born evil and dies evil. Nor can Aron manage change in his life: in fact, he cannot survive his fate. And Adam repeats his father's fate, although he recognizes the mistakes; it takes Abra and Lee standing over his deathbed to make him forgive Caleb.

DICHOTOMY OF GOOD AND EVIL

According to Steinbeck, all art concerns itself with just one story: "All novels, all poetry, are built n the never-ending contest in ourselves of good and evil."[8] At the beginning of this book, Steinbeck discusses what he thinks is the meaning of life and of death. He believes all men will ask at the end of their lives, if they have done good or evil. To illustrate his point, he tells the myth of Croesus, the richest man in the world. Croesus asks why he is not on the list of the luckiest men in the world. Solon, the wisest man in the world, replies it is because he is not yet dead, implying those who are dead are the luckiest because they no longer struggle with good and evil.

Steinbeck says the measure of a man is whether he was loved or hated after he has died. The best man is the man who tries to elevate men to dignity, bravery, and goodness when times are bad. When he dies, people are lost without him. Sam Hamilton is an example of such a man, because his son is lost without him.

A perfect illustration of the struggle between good and evil is the coexistence of churches and whorehouses. Steinbeck claims they are two sides of the same coin. A church could lift a man out of his sorrow and so could a whorehouse. The church was the center of the Salinas Valley's cultural life, from birth to death. The whorehouses were always there as well. Throughout history, brothels were accepted as a necessary evil.

Steinbeck concludes that people have individual responsibility to struggle with the forces of good and evil and to make of life what they will.

FATHERS

Although Adam realizes that Cyrus was a bad father, he repeats his mistakes. After Cathy shoots him and leaves, he falls into such a deep depression that he does not even notice his boys. He does not even bother to name them. It is Sam who shakes him out of his stupor. Sam physically and verbally assaults Adam and makes him name the twins. He also encourages Adam to resume planting his garden. When Adam protests, Sam tells him though things have changed for Adam, the garden will always be within him, and he has the power to create it on his ranch. Furthermore, Sam tells Adam about Cathy's new life, thereby shocking Adam. The death of Sam Hamilton is the catalyst that makes Adam change. He visits Cathy/Kate and realizes she no longer has an emotional hold on him. He is now free to live his life and to be a father to his boys. Even so, Adam favors Aron over Cal.

Sam Hamilton is portrayed as a wise and loving father, yet he failed to prepare his children for life without him. Sam Hamilton was the life of the family and, after his death, the family crumbles. Tom is unable to outlive the guilt he has about causing Dessie's death, so he commits suicide.

After Sam's death, Lee takes Sam's place in Adam's life. He continues giving him timely advice, including persuading him to forgive Cal at his deathbed. Although Lee is childless, he does the best job of being a father. He takes care of the twins when Adam is too depressed to notice them. As they grow, he gives them his full respect, without expecting adult reactions from them. He is always there to listen to them and offer counsel. He is the one who makes Cal realize he is not bad and that he has the will to change his life.

Steinbeck himself did not learn Adam's lesson. He always had a hard time showing love to his boys. He thought that writing this book would prove his love and alleviate brotherly rivalry between the boys. However, consider how Thom and John must have felt when they were old enough to understand the book. They were not sure which of them was supposed to be Cain and which Abel. It is true that Steinbeck wrote in his journals that he was concerned about Thom's well-being, meaning he thought Thom to be the Abel-like character. But the boys caused so much trouble growing up, they both seemed like Cains at times. Regardless, it is a rather strange legacy to leave to one's two sons: a novel in which only one son succeeds.

MYTH

Many critics felt that Steinbeck had lost his ability to write believable characters. Most agreed that the characters of Cathy, Lee, and Sam are in no way human. Yet some critics took it to mean that there is a symbolic level to the novel and that "[b]esides being individuals first and types second the characters are also something else– they are symbols."[9] In fact, in his diaries, Steinbeck wrote that he was trying to "emphasize symbolic meaning over narrative description."[10] It seems as if Steinbeck placed *East of Eden* in the middle of his spectrum between realism and allegory. *East of Eden* has very realistic concerns, such as Caleb's moral dilemma, but it also looms on a Biblical, or mythical level, with philosophical passages and characters that represent only one quality at a time. Cathy is a one-sided representation of evil. Sam Hamilton spouts goodness, wisdom, and reason. "Samuel's speech, attacked for being unrealistic, is elevated to the level of music to counterbalance the realistic narrative of the Trasks."[11] The character of Lee is more complicated than the first two. He is a benevolent sage like Sam, but he disguises himself as an immigrant. Unlike Sam, he does not seem to have a life of his own—he is planted at Adam's side, seemingly in order to help the Trask's survive. Lee is a mediator between the Trasks and their fate. His "specific role in the first half of East of Eden is the translator of the mythic into human terms."[12]

The first half of the novel is significantly more mythical than the second, with Cathy, the Moral Monster on the prowl, and Sam, the wise wizard. The second half is more down-to-earth; Sam is no longer present and Cathy's influence diminishes until it is gone. The second half takes a turn into more identifiable territory, as it focuses on Caleb's internal struggle.

PHALANX AND THE INDIVIDUAL

Steinbeck makes reference to the phalanx theory when he writes about the experience Adam has in the army. The army makes Adam much stronger and teaches him to no longer fear Charles. As the novel continues, however, Steinbeck puts the phalanx theory to rest. In this novel, he argues that it is the individual who is important, and not the group. Although the group makes people stronger, they must not lose their individuality. "Nothing was ever created by two men. There are no good collaborations whether in music, in art, in poetry, in mathematics, in philosophy . . . the group never invents anything."[13]

The ideal group in this novel is the family. Those who lack family are not leading the right kind of life (like Cathy and Charles). At the end of the novel, Caleb and Abra are about to start a family.

A WRITER WRITES AS HE LIVES

The Steinbecks arrived in Rome and received word that Elia Kazan, who had finished reading *East of Eden* in galley form, wanted to make a movie of it. *Viva Zapata* had recently been released in the United States and was enjoying great box-office success. Advance orders for *East of Eden* had reached more than 100,000 copies. The Book of the Month Club, however, did not release the book under its banner as it usually did, because of the controversial character of Cathy Trask.

Elia Kazan originally wanted Marlon Brando for the role of Cal in his film version of *East of Eden*, but then stumbled upon James Dean. When Steinbeck saw Dean, he told Kazan that Dean was a "snotty kid," but said he was right for the part, "sure as hell."[1] Kazan identified with the unlikable Caleb Trask who comes out on top, because he himself was being treated as an outcast for naming names to the HUAC in 1952. The film poster's tagline was: "Sometimes you can't tell who's good and who's bad!"—a message that both Kazan and Steinbeck could apply to their lives.[2]

While *East of Eden* jumped to the top of the best-seller list, the reviews, as usual, did not follow suit. *The New York Times* daily review by Oliver Prescott was truly a backhanded compliment: ". . .clumsy in structure and defaced by excessive melodramatics and much cheap sensationalism though it is, *East of Eden* is a serious, and, on the whole, a successful effort to grapple with a major theme."[3] And Leo Gurko in the *Nation* wrote, "This is the longest and most ambitious of the six novels by Steinbeck since the appearance of his masterpiece, *The Grapes of Wrath* . . . and raises the question of why Steinbeck's talent has declined so rapidly and so far."[4]

PRESIDENTIAL AFFAIRS

The reviews upset Steinbeck greatly, but he buried himself in working for Adlai Stevenson's presidential campaign against Dwight Eisenhower. He wrote many speeches and offered many ideas on campaigning. Few of Steinbeck's suggestions were taken. He was disappointed when Stevenson lost in 1952. For Steinbeck, Eisenhower represented all that was wrong with America. He once wrote to a friend: "How can I teach my boys the value and beauty of language . . . when the President himself reads

Westerns exclusively and cannot put together a simple English sentence?"[5]

Steinbeck was getting more involved with politics. He eventually became a good friend and supporter of President Lyndon Johnson. (Lady Bird Johnson and Elaine Scott had been college classmates in Texas.) He also wrote to Jacqueline Kennedy frequently during John Kennedy's presidency, and after Kennedy's death. For all of his shyness with the general public, Steinbeck truly enjoyed access to the famous and powerful. Perhaps, once again, he wanted to disprove his father's prediction about his amounting to nothing.

Ironically, Steinbeck was in the same position when it came to his sons as they got older. He had high expectations for the boys, but the boys felt they never could meet them. According to Nancy Steinbeck, John IV's wife: "The real issue at hand was his [Steinbeck's] refusal to let either son surpass him with their talent, wisdom, or courage. By dividing and conquering them with his favors, he rendered his sons impotent to grow beyond the parameters of what he would allow."[6]

SWEET THURSDAY MUSICAL

In 1953, John began work on a short play/novel, which he tentatively titled *Bear Flag*. Steinbeck was still trying to make a musical of *Cannery Row*, in addition to writing notes about all the people in Monterey. During the summer, Elaine took care of the boys and her daughter, Waverly. It was no easy task, complicated by John's frequent absence. She felt the boys resented her because of Gwyn's negative influence. In his autobiographical book, *The Other Side of Eden*, John IV makes the point that there was nowhere he could call home because he was driven crazy by his mother and had Elaine to contend with, whereas all he really wanted was the company of his father.

In September, John rented a house in Sag Harbor, on Long Island, New York. He liked being there because it reminded him of Monterey, and the people were ordinary and not put off by his celebrity. But when he returned to New York City, his anxiety about how *Bear Flag* would fare on Broadway seemed to overwhelm him. Steinbeck came down with a mysterious illness that caused him to spend ten days in the hospital. Elaine thought the illness was psychological in origin. But, in fact, it was discovered later Steinbeck had suffered a series of mini-strokes. Even though Steinbeck received the best of care from the finest New York doctors, there were no high-tech imaging machines at the time that might have found the problem. And there was no medication that might have prevented further strokes.

When the Steinbecks returned home, Oscar Hammerstein II called him and told him he had a deal. The title of the play had changed from *Bear Flag* to *At the Bear Flag Café* to *Sweet Thursday*, and finally, to *Pipe Dream*.

With very little on his plate to keep him in New York,

Steinbeck decided that he and Elaine should go to Europe. He thought he would keep a travel journal, and sell his observations to various travel and lifestyle magazines. John and Elaine headed first to Spain. While there, Steinbeck suffered from another series of strokes. He was informed in Spain that his heart was abnormally small to do the work for such a large body. After some rest, John and Elaine drove to Paris. They stayed in a very elegant apartment, where his neighbor was the president of France. In a letter to Oscar Hammerstein II, John mentioned how he, once a boy from Salinas, was overwhelmed to be a neighbor of the president of France and the famed Rothschild banking family. Then John received word that Richard Capa had been killed by a land mine in Vietnam. It immediately threw Steinbeck into another depression. With Ricketts and Capa gone and his health failing, Steinbeck began to contemplate his own mortality.

His gloom was brightened by the arrival of his boys. As Steinbeck proudly remarked, "they are like small men with incredible bodies and quick wits."[7] He also wrote to his psychiatrist as therapy for his depression. Moreover, the continuing adulation of the French public was a good antidote to his sadness.

While he was in France, Steinbeck learned *Sweet Thursday* had been published. The critics, once again, offered the usual array of reviews, such as *Sweet Thursday* was "like stuff that has been salvaged from the wastebasket."[8] Critics thought it was a reworking of *Tortilla Flat* and

Cannery Row. The plot features Doc (or Ed Ricketts), falling in and out of love with Suzy, a young prostitute from Monterey. At the end of the story, Doc and Suzy finally reunite and there is a big party. It was a perfect plot for a Broadway musical.

The Steinbecks spent Christmas in New York, with all the parties and trimmings, and, in January, they welcomed the Southern writer William Faulkner to their home. Unfortunately, Faulkner was drunk and sullen most of the time, and it was not a pleasant experience for anyone. A few months later, Faulkner, this time sober, offered his apologies to the Steinbecks.

Steinbeck bought a home in Sag Harbor in February. He proceeded at once to redesign and repair it. He also bought a new boat. He worked on the house through the spring. It was good therapy for him.

In April, through his relationship with Elizabeth Otis, Steinbeck met with Norman Cousins, the distinguished publisher of the *Saturday Review*. Steinbeck developed a very close relationship with Cousins, and he became an editor-at-large at the magazine. He contributed many articles, on such topics as the role of the United Nations and on juvenile delinquency. Steinbeck was a good essayist and journalist, and his work was well-received. After a relaxing summer in their house in Sag Harbor, John and Elaine returned to New York in anticipation of the Broadway opening of *Pipe Dream*. The critics had panned it in its Boston opening. Steinbeck felt the characters were not "earthy" enough. "You've turned my prostitute into a visiting nurse," he wrote to Hammerstein.[9] *Pipe Dream* opened on Broadway at the end of November to lukewarm reviews. Had it not had an advance sale of one million dollars, the show would have closed before it reached two hundred and forty-six performances. For Steinbeck, it was the end of his playwriting experience.

PIPPIN

John decided to write a satirical novel about an individual who would become king, indicating intellectuals did not make good politicians. This became *The Short Reign of Pippin IV*. After the Christmas holidays, the Steinbecks, as was their regular habit, went south. They rented a yacht and cruised the Windward and Leeward islands in the Caribbean in January. In February, the well-rested Steinbecks returned to Sag Harbor, where the house had been winterized. Steinbeck wanted to concentrate on his Pippin novel and needed the solitude of Sag Harbor.

John also wrote a short story, which appeared in the March issue of *The Atlantic Monthly*. It was called "How Mr. Hogan Robbed A Bank," and would reemerge as *The Winter of Our Discontent*, Steinbeck's last novel. Set in a fictitious New England town, the story revolves around the moral downfall of Ethan Hawley, a descendant of Pilgrims, a Harvard grad, and one-time successful business owner who's down on his luck, as he succumbs to his family's insistent cries for a comfortable life. Ethan's tale was meant to symbolize the general degeneration of

American morals after World War II due to materialism or conspicuous consumption.

That summer, John and Elaine were once again hosts to John IV and Thom in Sag Harbor where Elaine's daughter, Waverly, was to be married. Elaine was very busy taking care of arrangements and this time John had to take care of the boys who were growing more delinquent as they got older.

POLITICAL INVOLVEMENT

On August 10, 1956, the Steinbecks flew to Chicago where John was to cover the Democratic Presidential Convention. At a small political dinner, they met Adlai Stevenson, the front-runner for the nomination. Steinbeck was very impressed with the man. He also became fascinated with the political rituals of the party and the campaign. He felt the Republican Convention in California was far less exciting because there were no surprises about who was going to run: President Eisenhower and Vice President Nixon were renominated. Throughout his coverage of the Chicago Democratic Convention, John wrote little anecdotes about the people he observed. He enjoyed the people he was meeting and the writing, but was becoming exhausted. At the end, he hoped he would never have to do another convention. Steinbeck ended up writing many speeches for Stevenson and his staff, but again Stevenson lost the election.

In late November, Steinbeck joined a program with

other writers called "People to People." It was created so that American artists could visit behind The Iron Curtain to make contact with their peers. The committee also fought for the release of the writer Ezra Pound who was imprisoned at St. Elizabeth's Hospital in Washington, D.C., for giving aid to the Nazis during World War II. Steinbeck felt this was not the job of the writers' committee, and although Pound was released, Steinbeck felt the committee had lost credibility because it would not entertain more serious political questions, such as why the United States had not supported the Hungarian revolutionaries in 1956.

During the winter, Steinbeck began work on a modern English version of Malory's *Knights of the Round Table*. He found original documents at the Morgan Library and enjoyed uncovering new material. Steinbeck believed Malory might have gone to Italy as a soldier of fortune. Steinbeck decided he had to go to Italy to find some proof that his suspicion was correct. With Elaine and his favorite sister, Mary, Steinbeck sailed on March 25, 1957, to Naples. John wrote articles for the *Courier-Journal*, as well as the *Saturday Review* and *Holiday* magazine, to help defray the costs of this trip.

Steinbeck went to the Vatican Library, a resource of centuries of manuscripts. Because of his association with the United States Information Service, Steinbeck was allowed to visit many libraries that were unavailable to the general public and to writers at large. John believed through this research he could get a better feel for what

Malory was really like. Steinbeck believed Malory's *Morte d'Arthur* was one of the greatest novels in the English language. He thought Malory the novelist, and Lancelot, the main character, were one and the same.

While Steinbeck searched for Malory, *The Short Reign of Pippin IV* was published. Steinbeck wanted Pippin to be a great epic like *The Grapes of Wrath*. But he was far removed from that era, just as he was far removed from Monterey. The book sold well, in spite of the poor reviews. In the end, it remains the least popular of Steinbeck's novels. *The Short Reign of Pippin IV* imagines what would happen if the monarchy were restored to France. Basically, Steinbeck wanted to compare Americans and the French. The negative aspects of American materialism emerged as a new theme in Steinbeck's work and would run through *The Winter of Our Discontent* and *Travels With Charley*.

HUAC, AGAIN

In May, the Steinbecks went to Florence. John was distressed to learn that Arthur Miller, the playwright, had been indicted by the House Committee on Un-American Activities for refusing to testify. Steinbeck wrote an essay published in the June 1957 *Esquire* magazine in which he condemns the HUAC and defends Arthur Miller. In the essay, he compares the HUAC to Russia, where "we have been revolted by the Soviet Union's encouragement of spying and telling, children reporting their parents, and wives informing on their husbands. In Hitler's Germany, it was considered patriotic to report your friends and relations to the proper authorities. And we in America have felt safe from and superior to these things. But are we so safe and superior?"[10] He wrote to Pat Covici that too many artists were cowards for not standing up for "Artie" and that he felt "a lonely sorrow and shame" for waiting so long to defend him.[11]

ABANDONED PROJECTS

Steinbeck could never avoid the voice of literary critics. This time, it was a review by Alfred Kazin of a book about Steinbeck. Kazin had nothing good to say about Steinbeck and called his later writings "cute and sentimental."[12] What was worse was that this review appeared on the front page of *The New York Times Book Review*, and thus received wide attention. At first, Steinbeck was not bothered. He was used to this kind of criticism, but then he received letters from Pat Covici and Harold Greenberg who were furious. It bothered Steinbeck, so late in his career, to be treated this way.

Steinbeck returned to Sag Harbor and worked on the Malory material every day for a month. Then he put it aside to work on an idea he had about a modern-day Don Quixote, which he would call *Don Keehan*. He wrote to Henry Fonda to let him know he was writing the character with him in mind. He remained at Sag Harbor, working into the fall. But he felt he was getting nowhere on this project. In December, he abandoned it. The

Henry Fonda (center) in a scene from the film version of John Steinbeck's *The Grapes of Wrath*. Steinbeck's aborted project *Don Keehan* was written with Fonda in mind.

negative criticism from Alfred Kazin had hit a nerve with Steinbeck. He knew he had to write something to convince himself, if not the critics. He decided he had to get away from America and all its external pressure.

At the end of February 1958, the Steinbecks closed down their home in Sag Harbor, and sailed to England. The filmmaker Robert Bolt had rented a home for them in Somerset, and John and Elaine were very happy. Elaine was overjoyed with her husband's response to his new environment. On the last day of April, the Steinbecks visited "Camelot," the place where King Arthur supposedly held court. This dream-like existence could not last for long. John IV was having trouble in school and Waverly was in the process of a divorce. These pieces of news made Steinbeck immerse himself further into his writing, but no matter what he did, the writing was not going smoothly. He sent a few chapters to Pat Covici and Elizabeth Otis, but their responses were not encouraging. When he got to the point in the book where Sir Lancelot decides to have a physical relationship with Guinevere, thereby betraying Arthur, he could not write it.

In August, Steinbeck decided to shelve the Malory book once more and spend some time with his friends, the Wallsteins. They set off for Wales, in search of Arthurian relics. By mid-October, Steinbeck realized his quest for Arthur and his vision for writing a new translation of Malory were coming to nothing. He decided to close up the Somerset home.

FAILING HEALTH

When they came home to New York, Elaine noticed certain changes in John that were troubling. One day, she smelled something burning. She ran up to his room. He was unconscious, and the cigarette he was smoking had fallen out of his fingers and ignited the mattress and his pajamas. Elaine quickly put out the fire, and called an ambulance. John had suffered another small stroke, and the attack signaled the final downward turn in Steinbeck's health.

The Malory experience had depressed Steinbeck and his recovery was slow. For weeks afterward, even until Christmas, his speech was uncertain and he temporarily lost the agility in his fingers. He wrote to Elizabeth Otis that he was going to rest for a while. But that was next to impossible for Steinbeck. During that period he said to Elia Kazan: "I have nothing to write about anymore . . . The job of a writer is to tell about his time. I've been too concerned with what's past . . . I've also lost touch with the country. I don't know what's happening out there anymore."[13]

Soon after the New Year, Steinbeck began work on *The Winter of Our Discontent*. This novel emerged as a result of his failure to write the Malory book and his disappointment with the moral decay and materialism of Americans. He also continued to write articles for *Saturday Review*, *Esquire*, and *Holiday*. In March, he wrote to the *Courier-Journal* that he wanted to do a series of articles under the byline of "The Old Curmudgeon."

Steinbeck also received letters from well-known universities asking if he would like them to bestow an honorary degree upon him. That made Steinbeck very angry. He never got a degree from Stanford. Why should he accept a fake degree at ceremonies where he did not wish to be and did not wish to speak?

ANOTHER AMERICAN JOURNEY

Steinbeck wrote through the spring and expected he would finish *The Winter of Our Discontent* during the summer of 1959. He decided that as soon as he finished the novel, he would take off and learn about his country. He would travel by pickup truck, with a room inside the truck. He wanted to go alone and just listen to the sounds of America and the voice of Americans. He did not want anyone to recognize him, he just wanted to record what America was all about. He felt he did not know it anymore. This idea originally came from Elizabeth Otis, who thought this "journey" would put Steinbeck in contact with ordinary Americans and perhaps restore his faith in America. The idea of all this frightened Elaine. She felt Steinbeck was not healthy enough for this trip.

Meanwhile Steinbeck was still working on *The Winter Of Our Discontent*, which was to be set in Sag Harbor. But he kept very quiet about it. As "The Old Curmudgeon," he sent a letter to Adlai Stevenson in which he said that Americans' lack of morality was in direct relation to having or wanting too many things. "If I wanted to destroy a nation, I would give it too much, and have it on its knees; miserable, greedy, and sick."[14] The letter was leaked to the press and there was a minor furor. People argued on both sides. The revered poet Carl Sandburg said, "Anything John Steinbeck says about this country should be listened to. His record of love for his country and service for it is such that what he says is important."[15] John completed a draft of *The Winter of Our Discontent* and sent it to Elizabeth Otis in July. Stevenson suggested that Steinbeck make a cross-country trip, much as he himself had been doing during his campaigns, to rediscover America. And so John hopped in a truck with Elaine's poodle, Charley, on September 23, 1959. He was going to check on the pulse of Americans and, of course, he wanted to prove to himself and everyone else that he could still take care of himself.

The book, *Travels with Charley*, opens with Steinbeck's experience with Hurricane Donna, one of the worst hurricanes to hit the East Coast. He describes how the storm was pushing his boat, the *Fayre Elayne*, out to sea. This was one possession Steinbeck did not want to lose. So he jumped into the water, swam to the boat, got in, started it, and anchored it in the bay. It was quite a feat for Steinbeck, considering his physical weakness.

In his travels he revealed his sense of ecology, long before there were environmentalists. He commented that at every town he visited, a town dump loaded with car wrecks and debris of all kinds always greeted him. He thought Americans had lost their souls, especially in trailer parks, where he noted the lowest rung of people lived. He thought trailer park people were alien and could not typify mainstream America. He traveled up and down Route 90 to Chicago and then headed west. In one phone call to Elaine, she mentioned to him that his chatty letters reminded her of Robert Louis Stevenson's *Travels with a*

Donkey. And that's how Steinbeck came to call his book *Travels with Charley*.

John met Elaine in Seattle and they drove south to California to visit John's sisters, Esther and Beth. After a visit with Elaine's family, John drove to New Orleans to witness for himself how the schools there were being integrated. He stood on the sidelines and watched young white mothers spit and jeer at the tiny black children who were going to school. No one recognized him. He told them he was from England, and bystanders told him the whole integration business was the fault of the Jews. He returned to Sag Harbor. He had completed his trip in eleven weeks.

Steinbeck immediately set to work writing *Travels with Charley*, based on the copious notes he had taken during the trip. He felt quite good that this mission was completed with very little harm done to his health.

Steinbeck attended the 1961 inauguration of President John F. Kennedy with his friend John Galbraith. He wrote to President Kennedy to let him know how impressed he was with his speech, and received a follow-up note from the President, with apologies for not having had the chance to meet Steinbeck personally.

After the presidential inauguration, John and Elaine flew to Barbados for a vacation. Steinbeck was not comfortable on the island because of the division between rich and poor. He mostly stayed in his room and worked on *Travels with Charley*.

THE END OF FICTION

When John and Elaine arrived home on March 4, Thom and John IV were sitting on their doorstep. They had both had enough of their mother. According to Nancy Steinbeck, John IV's "mother physically and emotionally abused him after the divorce, she would wake him in the middle of the night by smashing scotch bottles on his head . . . sobbing she would say 'It's all your fault. If you and your brother hadn't been born, I'd still be married to your father.'"[16] John and Elaine took them in. However, Elaine was left to deal with the boys by herself once again because John was scheduled to leave for Mexico to cover a scientific expedition for *Life* magazine.

Steinbeck returned to Sag Harbor with Elaine in mid-April 1961, while the boys returned to boarding school. He continued working on *Travels with Charley*. He did write to Pat Covici that he thought the writing was "formless." Nonetheless, *Holiday* magazine published excerpts from *Travels with Charley* to much acclaim. In June *The Winter of Our Discontent* was published. The latter is a story of a basically good man who becomes distressed at the way America and Americans were turning out to be greedy and amoral. Most of the reviews were lukewarm, although one reviewer for *The Atlantic* wrote "not since *The Grapes of Wrath* had he managed such natural and realistic conversation."[17] Ironically, Steinbeck was depressed because he realized all the critics, good and bad, always came back to *The Grapes of Wrath*, as if he could never grow any further as a writer. *The Winter of Our Discontent* was the

141

last novel Steinbeck would write. He was finished with fiction.

AN EXTENDED TRIP WITH THE BOYS

As his peers and friends died, Steinbeck thought more and more about his relationship with John IV and Thom. He decided he wanted to give them a gift that would be a legacy for them and their heirs. It would be an extended sailing trip. His plan was to take Thom, John IV, Elaine, and a tutor and travel around the world slowly for an entire year. This was an ambitious undertaking. The tutor was Terrence McNally, who later would become a well-known playwright. The Steinbecks invited McNally to Sag Harbor so he could get to know the boys. On the day they set sail, McNally had a sense of foreboding. Steinbeck drew up an extensive but flexible itinerary from England to Italy, to Egypt, to Japan, to Australia, and parts in-between, and finally back to San Francisco.

They sailed to England first and McNally was amazed at how much Steinbeck knew. But Elaine was noticing friction between Thom and Terrence. It seemed both Thom and John IV thought of this trip as a vacation, which they did not want spoiled by any schoolwork. This caused major arguments between Steinbeck and the boys. After England, they went on to France and then Italy. On November 25, in a hotel in Italy, Thom got into a fight that angered Steinbeck. Then, in a split second, Steinbeck fell unconscious. The boys stopped fighting, left him with McNally, and ran for help. The doctor could not tell if it was a heart attack or a stroke. Once again, Steinbeck recovered. While John and Elaine headed for Rome where John was to have a special audience with Pope John Paul XXIII on Christmas Eve, Terrence took the boys around Northern Italy. They all met in Rome for Christmas.

In spite of a very pleasant reunion with the boys, Steinbeck's health was still very shaky, and it was made worse by the news of the death of Harold Guinzburg, his publisher. Elaine and John decided he could not endure an entire world tour. The boys and Terrence went around the Mediterranean, while Elaine and John stayed on the Isle of Capri. John busied himself with the galleys of *Travels with Charley*. Between April and May, John and Elaine joined the rest of the Steinbeck contingent in Positano, Italy, and finally returned to New York in late May, after touring the Greek Islands.

CHAPTER 10

THE MEASURE OF THIS MAN

The return to Sag Harbor for Elaine and John coincided with the publication of *Travels with Charley*. This time, there were some good reviews. *The New York Times* said it was "a pure delight." *Newsweek* called it "highly entertaining."[1] And the *Atlantic Monthly* said, "This is a book which should be read slowly for its savor; and one which, like Thoreau, will be quoted and measured by our own experience."[2] *Travels with Charley* moved to the top of the bestseller list almost immediately.

THE NOBEL PRIZE

One night in late October 1962, John was watching television and suddenly heard that he had won the Nobel Prize for Literature. He and Elaine started dancing. Phones began ringing, and John called the boys. Thom's reaction to his father's honor was quite interesting: "If the whole world says he's such a great man, who am I to argue with them? If his opinion means that much and he gets the Nobel Prize for it, then when he tells me I'm full of it, he must be right."[3] The next day, there were seventy-five reporters and cameramen, waiting to meet with Steinbeck. They asked many questions, to which Steinbeck replied as best as he could. He said, "This prize is a monster,"[4] which referred to the fact that many writers who received the Nobel Prize never wrote again. For Steinbeck, the reaction by his critics to his winning was difficult to handle.

The New York Times wrote that, while they did not want to detract from the honor Steinbeck received, "perhaps a poet or critic or historian—whose significance, influence, and sheer body of work had already made a more profound impression on the literature of our age," should have won.[5] While John was trying to calm his family and his friends, telling them the comment was not important, it certainly was. His constant battle with the critics had reached its lowest point. John wondered why the awards of previous Nobel Prize winners were never questioned. Steinbeck felt unfairly singled out. He tried to put that aside in favor of the many congratulatory messages from around the world.

John, Elaine, and Alice Guinzburg, the widow of Harold Guinzburg, flew to Sweden on December 8. No sooner did they deplane, than they were praised and feted at many dinners and luncheons given by the Swedish government, Steinbeck's Swedish publisher, and the United States Embassy, to name a few.

Steinbeck's Nobel speech was short but powerful. It was not likely he would have a platform as prestigious as this one again, and he chose his words very carefully. While he was honored to receive the award, Steinbeck said he did not want to speak as a "grateful and apologetic mouse, but to roar like a lion out of my pride in my profession." He referred to his critics as "an emasculated critical priesthood singing their litanies in empty churches."[6] Then he mapped out the role of the writer in the age of the Cold War. He encouraged writers to write about man's worthy aspirations but warned them not to ignore the power of man who had reached God-like proportions. Man now had the power to destroy the entire earth. It was the responsibility of the writers to point this out in all its ramifications through their literature. He acknowledged the irony that the giver of the prize, Alfred Nobel, was himself responsible for the production of explosives in the United States.

The Steinbecks came home a few days before Christmas. But even that holiday could not be enjoyed completely. Arthur Mizener, another critic who did not think Steinbeck should receive the Nobel Prize, weighed in. In his essay, he says after *The Grapes of Wrath*, "most serious readers" had stopped reading Steinbeck because of his sentimentality.[7]

Once again, Steinbeck was furious. Yet other writers saw the injustice of these persistent criticisms. Gore Vidal,

Nobel Prize winners at the 1962 ceremony (from left to right): Maurice Wilkins (physiology or medicine), Max Perutz (chemistry), Francis Crick (physiology or medicine), John Steinbeck, James Watson (physiology or medicine), and John Kendrew (chemistry).

an American author, said critics like Mizener and Alfred Kazin "believe that good literature is written for a small, select group of people like themselves. They could never forgive Steinbeck for saying things that people wanted and needed to hear."[8]

Steinbeck sold his Seventy-Second Street brownstones (which had become burdensome for him) and moved to a very large, luxury apartment in a brand-new building a few blocks away.

147

BACK IN THE USSR

In the spring of 1963, Steinbeck was asked to join a cultural exchange between America and Russia to help soften their relationship during the Cold War. Previously the poet Robert Frost had participated. Steinbeck asked if he could bring some of the younger contingent of writers, like Edward Albee and Terrence McNally, the Steinbeck boys' tutor.

In early May, Elaine and John moved back to Sag Harbor, where John suffered a detached retina that nearly blinded him. He spent the whole summer in bed without moving his head, while some of his friends, including the writer John O'Hara, read to him. In September, when he was fully recovered, John and Elaine went to Washington, D.C., for a briefing on his trip to Moscow. There, he met with President Kennedy.

In Moscow, the exchange group met up with Edward Albee, who had taken on the role of speaking with dissident Soviet writers. He believed Steinbeck was too imposing a figure and that they would feel more comfortable speaking with someone of their generation.

From September to November, the Steinbecks traveled all over Russia, meeting up with Albee from time to time. All through the trip, someone from the Soviet Writers' Union accompanied them. They thought he must have been a spy. Wherever they went, people always knew the Steinbecks, and some had even read *The Winter of Our Discontent*, without, of course, having paid any royalties to Steinbeck.

When they arrived in Leningrad on November 8, Steinbeck collapsed and was hospitalized for tests. The doctors determined John was not seriously ill, but exhausted. They recommended three weeks of rest. Steinbeck would not hear of it. Within one day of his release from the hospital, Steinbeck was lecturing at Leningrad State University.

On November 15, the Steinbecks left for Poland. They were in Warsaw on November 22, 1963, when President Kennedy was assassinated. It was a tumultuous time for Steinbeck. He and Elaine flew to Vienna to attend a memorial service. Everywhere they went, people offered their sympathies. They returned to the United States in December and immediately flew to Washington, D.C., for a debriefing. Later they had dinner at the White House with the new president, Lyndon Johnson. Lady Bird Johnson and Elaine renewed their acquaintance from their college days at the University of Texas. The Johnsons and the Steinbecks would remain good friends.

MORE TROUBLE WITH THE BOYS

Back in New York for Christmas, John and Elaine finally had time to relax in their new apartment overlooking Seventy-Second Street. Thom and John IV were there and it was quite a celebration. They saw the boys off at the station to return to school. Everything seemed to be fine until they got a phone call from the school's headmaster.

Thom and John IV had not shown up. They were finally found at Gwyn's house, a previously used trick. They complained they could not get close to their father and that he was drunk and always depressed. Terrence McNally noted that John could not get as close to the boys as he wanted to and Gwyn just made it worse by saying such awful things about him.

Then Gwyn sued to get more money from John for child support. The boys took Gwyn's side. John wondered if they even appreciated the trip they had recently taken with him. Elaine and John had to appear in court with Gwyn. The judge awarded Gwyn a very small increase. The judge noted that if John had not been as famous, the hearing would never have been held. Gwyn, severely disappointed, left the courtroom in tears.

That summer, when the boys were visiting, they explained they had to go along with their mother even though they did not want to. John accepted their explanation. According to Elaine, "he loved them very much, but he could not understand their behavior."[9] The gap between the boys and Steinbeck would never be bridged. Another generation of father and son(s) could not accommodate each other. Personal history could not be prevented from repeating itself.

THE PRESIDENTIAL MEDAL

Elaine and John moved back to Sag Harbor for the summer of 1964. It was there they learned John was to receive the Presidential Medal of Freedom in a ceremony that September. The rest of the time John spent analyzing what he had accomplished in his life at the age of sixty-two. What bothered him the most was that he thought his time had already passed. He noted in a letter to Pat Covici, "more and more, young people look at me in amazement because they thought I was dead."[10] At the award ceremony was Pat Covici, who had a big part, from the beginning, in making this event a reality. It was the last time Pat and John saw each other. Covici died on October 14.

AMERICA AND AMERICANS

As if to give John a reason for working, Tom Guinzburg, who was then running Viking, sent him a set of photographs for which he needed commentary. The pictures were of typical Americans being American, á la *Travels with Charley*. The book would be called *America and Americans*. Steinbeck enjoyed writing this commentary. He did not feel bound to a specific audience. He was writing for himself, and the words came easily. In the middle of it, John learned that his favorite sister, Mary Steinbeck Dekker, had died.

America and Americans was published in 1966, while the Steinbecks were on a trip to Israel. Many of the columns Steinbeck wrote seemed to pave the way for this book. Some critics dismissed it as a book for show. One critic, Richard E. Peterson, described *America and*

Americans as a reflection of all of Steinbeck's works because of its emphasis on the waste Americans have made of America, and his hopes that Americans would return to its vision of principle and purpose.[11]

Newsday Columns

Between drafts of *America and Americans*, Steinbeck worked on a series of columns for *Newsday*, under the title of "Letters to Alicia," in honor of Harry F. Guggenheim's late wife, Alice. One of his more controversial columns was about a forty-eight-page manuscript he and Professor Vinnaver, of Manchester University, had discovered at Alnwick Castle while he was there in November. The manuscript began with a list of Kings and concluded with the death of King Arthur. The British press picked up on the column and exaggerated the importance of what Steinbeck and Vinnaver had found. The press claimed it was a genuine Malory manuscript. This undermined the credibility of Steinbeck, and especially of Vinnaver, who had promised Steinbeck he would help him in any way he could. Steinbeck and Vinnaver never claimed the manuscript was an original Malory, but it seemed that way to historians.

Another *Newsday* column was about John and Elaine's visit to Israel. Steinbeck wrote that he admired the willpower and endurance of Israel in spite of the fact it was "this little area of the world." He contrasted Israel's energetic self-image with the apathy and moral decay in the United States.

VIETNAM

John and Elaine were, once again, guests at the White House, where John met Jack Valenti, who was an adviser to President Johnson; they would become friends. President Johnson was always seeking support from Steinbeck for the war in Vietnam. Steinbeck was a staunch supporter of Johnson, but not as strong a supporter of the war. After John IV decided to enlist, Steinbeck's support for the war increased. In fact, President Johnson invited John and John IV to the White House in May 1966, for which John was very grateful. Steinbeck had thought if Stevenson had been President the war in Vietnam might not have occurred.

With John IV's enlistment, the war in Vietnam hit closer to home for Steinbeck. He began to look at the war from the perspective of the ordinary soldier who was doing his patriotic duty. He supported the troops, thinking of them as victims, as well as heroes, similar to how he positioned the Joad family in *The Grapes of Wrath*.

While Steinbeck would continue to support President Johnson, his doubts about the war grew, but he stayed quiet. Even after John IV wrote to him that he thought the war was a grave error, Steinbeck continued to remain silent. What he wrote to his friend Jack Valenti was different, but it would not be made public until after the war and Steinbeck's death. He was sure that the war was a huge mistake.

Harry Guggenheim suggested Steinbeck become a correspondent for *Newsday* with his first-hand observations of Vietnam and the war. Steinbeck was interested. He had been asked by President Johnson's staff to do the same thing months before but did not follow up because he did not want his observations to be tainted if anyone thought he was on President Johnson's payroll. Another reason Steinbeck expressed an interest was that John IV was there. Elaine would come with him. Steinbeck believed she was indispensable to his well-being.

Steinbeck, accompanied by Major Sam Gipson, got right into the action in Vietnam. He relayed to Harry Guggenheim how the ground war was being fought. Guns and mines were easily hidden in the jungle, and it was tricky to get around. Steinbeck felt as if he were back in his World War II days. He commented that the Viet Cong soldiers who were captured were strong and brave. One night, Steinbeck was allowed to accompany John IV's unit. As John IV relates it, he quickly flew to his combat station, armed with an M-79 grenade. Steinbeck had an M-60 machine gun. "I saw my father behind some sandbags overlooking my position, with his M-60 ready. . . . And what an amazing feeling to see him ready in his flack jacket and helmet protecting my back . . . it had been enough to bring us to a brief moment of . . . awareness for each other . . . I felt a brotherly love in my heart."[12]

Steinbeck concluded that most of the soldiers did not

want to be there but felt an obligation to their country. Steinbeck did not wish to comment politically; that was as far as he went. John Steinbeck remained loyal to President Johnson and to the country. At this point much of the nation was regretting American involvement in the war. Many felt that Steinbeck had sold out and betrayed his liberal past. *Newsday* cancelled his column.

AILING HEALTH

Steinbeck had covered a great deal of territory in his visit to Vietnam, and by the end of February, when they finally arrived at an air-conditioned hotel, Steinbeck's body gave out. He was in bed for four days. When he felt better, he and Elaine flew to Kyoto to meet up with John IV, who was on leave. All three had a good time. However, when John and Elaine arrived in Tokyo, John was, once again, in agony. He had three crushed discs in his spine, it was discovered, and he was in excruciating pain.

By the time summer rolled around, John and Elaine were back in Sag Harbor. He was depressed about his pain, about the futility of winning the war in Vietnam, and was frustrated about not letting President Johnson know what he was really thinking.

For Steinbeck, it was a period of time when the words did not flow easily. He was scheduled to have surgery on his back that October. But a few days before the surgery, John got a phone call from *Newsweek* magazine for his comments about the arrest of his son John IV on drug charges. John IV was back from Vietnam and was working at the Army Information Office at the Pentagon. The police confiscated twenty pounds of marijuana when they went to his apartment. While John IV was acquitted of all charges, the intervening time between jail and the trial did not help to improve the relationship with his father, nor with Thom. Although just months before they were in battle side by side, Steinbeck decided never to speak to John IV again.

According to Elaine, the boys became resentful of their father as they grew older. Perhaps they resented his relationship with Elaine. Although John loved them deeply, he did not know how to express that love. He wrote an epic for them, rather than spending time with them. The boys had few of the responsibilities and emotional securities of most children and continued to act recklessly. Steinbeck's wealth left them financially stable. But it would be difficult for them to live up to their father's reputation.

Steinbeck's back operation left him extremely weak. All he could do was stay in bed and read. Right before Christmas 1967, John and Elaine flew to Grenada, and rented a cottage where John could recuperate. The sun always had a positive effect on John, and he was sure it would still work for him. They stayed until the end of January, and then returned to Sag Harbor. Unfortunately, the Caribbean sun had not worked for John. He continued to feel weak. They had to return to their apartment in the city where the doctors and hospitals were in easy reach.

Steinbeck's physician at this time was Denton Cox. Along with his medical record sent to Dr. Cox, John included a note in which he explained that he had no fear of dying, and that he enjoyed a "good span of life."[13] Steinbeck wanted Dr. Cox to refrain from telling Elaine anything that would cause her pain or sorrow. Steinbeck, it seems, was aware that his time was coming to a close.

John felt miserable in the city. He and Elaine moved back to Sag Harbor. But John suffered another small stroke as well as a minor heart attack. At the request of Dr. Cox, John returned to the city, where he stayed in a hospital, under close observation, for three weeks. But as soon as he was released, he insisted on going back to Sag Harbor. He needed to be near the water. In November, John's breathing became more difficult. He was suffering from emphysema and hardening of the arteries.

LAST BREATHS

Steinbeck had many visitors at home including Thom and John IV, and Elizabeth Otis. One day he was reading about a new procedure called a heart bypass. This surgery was in its infancy in 1968. He asked Dr. Cox to send some cardiologists to the apartment to examine him as a possible candidate. When they told him nothing could be done because of his other complications, he apologized for having taken their time.

On the morning of December 20, 1968, Elaine knew John did not have very long to live. Many of his friends visited that day. Elaine slipped into bed with John where they both reminisced about the best times they had. Elaine fell asleep and when she woke, John was dead. He took his last breath at 5:30 that afternoon.[14] He died simply, perhaps with some regrets, but surrounded with love. The man who could capture the sound and the heart of ordinary people, who could depict a singular desolate time in America, who had hopes and dreams for his country, who was a journalist and a friend, was silenced. His kind would not be heard from again. His ashes are buried in the Hamilton Family Plot, at the Garden of Memories Cemetery of Salinas.

CHRONOLOGY

1902—Born February 27, to Olive Hamilton and John Ernst Steinbeck II in Salinas, California, the third of four children.

1915–1919—Attends Salinas High School.

1919–1925—Attends Stanford University, without receiving a degree.

1925—Works as a laborer and as a journalist for the *New York American* in New York City.

1926–1928—Works as a caretaker at a summer home in Lake Tahoe, California.

1929—McBride publishes *Cup of Gold*.

1930—Marries Carol Henning.
Meets Edward F. Ricketts.

1932—*The Pastures of Heaven* is published.

1933—*To A God Unknown* is published.

1934—Mother dies.

1935—Tortilla Flat is published.

1936—Father dies.
In Dubious Battle is published.

1937—*Of Mice and Men* and *The Red Pony* are published.
The play, *Of Mice and Men*, opens in New York.

1938—*Their Blood Is Strong* is published.
The play, *Of Mice and Men*, is awarded the New York Drama Critics Circle Award.

The Long Valley is published.

1939—*The Grapes of Wrath* is published.
The film, *Of Mice and Men*, is released.

1940—The film, *The Grapes of Wrath*, is released.
Makes marine expedition in the Gulf of California with Ed Ricketts.
Awarded the National Book Award and the Pulitzer Prize for *The Grapes of Wrath*.
Works on documentary film about living conditions in rural Mexico, *The Forgotten Village*.

1941—*Sea of Cortez* (written with Ed Ricketts) is published.

1942—Divorces Carol.
The Moon Is Down is published.
Bombs Away is published.
The play, *The Moon Is Down*, opens in New York.
The film, *Tortilla Flat*, is released.

1943—The film, *The Moon Is Down*, is released.
Marries Gwyn Conger.
Works as a war correspondent for the *New York Herald Tribune* in Europe and North Africa.

1944—Writes screenplay for Alfred Hitchcock's *Lifeboat*.
First son, Thom, is born on August 2.

1945—*Cannery Row* is published.

1946—Second son, John IV, is born on June 12.

1947—*The Wayward Bus* is published.
The Pearl is published.
Tours Russia with photographer Robert Capa, for the *New York Herald Tribune*.

1948—*A Russian Journal* is published.
Ed Ricketts is killed in an automobile accident.
Divorces Gwyn.
Elected to American Academy of Arts and Letters.

1950—*Burning Bright* is published.
The play, *Burning Bright*, opens in New York.
Marries Elaine Anderson Scott.

1951—*The Log from the Sea of Cortez* is published.

1952—The film, *Viva Zapata!*, is released.
East of Eden is published.

1954—*Sweet Thursday* is published.

1955—Purchases a summer home in Sag Harbor, Long Island.
Pipe Dream, a musical version of *Sweet Thursday*, opens in New York.

1957—*The Short Reign of Pippin IV* is published.
The film, *The Wayward Bus*, is released.

1958—*Once There Was a War* is published.

1959—Tours England and Wales, researching background for a modern English version of Malory's *Morte d'Arthur*.

1960—Tours United States with his poodle, Charley.

1961—*The Winter of Our Discontent* is published.

1962—*Travels with Charley* is published.
Awarded the Nobel Prize for Literature.

1963—Tours Scandinavia, Eastern Europe, and Russia on United States Information Agency cultural mission.

1964—Awarded United States Medal of Freedom by President Lyndon B. Johnson.

1965—Writes articles for *Newsday* from Vietnam.

1966—*America and Americans* is published.

1968—Dies of arteriosclerosis in New York City, December 20.

Chapter Notes

Chapter 1. Roots of a Writer

1. John Steinbeck, *East of Eden* (New York: The Viking Press, 1952), p. 5.

2. Jay Parini, *John Steinbeck, A Biography* (New York: Henry Holt & Company, 1995), p. 13.

3. Ibid., p.13.

4. Ibid., p. 15.

5. Jackson J. Benson, *The True Adventures of John Steinbeck, Writer* (New York: Penguin Books, 1984), p. 21.

6. Ibid.

7. Ibid., p. 24.

8. Parini, p. 18.

9. Benson, pp. 58–60.

10. Parini, p. 35.

11. "Pigasus," *Center for Steinbeck Studies*, n.d., <http://www2.sjsu.edu/steinbeck/Biography/Pigasus.htm> (December 13, 2003).

12. Parini, p. 42.

13. Thomas Kiernan, *The Intricate Music: A Biography of John Steinbeck* (Boston: Little Brown and Company, 1970), pp. 104–107.

14. Parini, pp. 53–54.

15. Benson, pp. 98–99.

16. Parini, pp. 56–57.

17. Benson, p. 113.

18. Ibid., pp. 133–134.

19. Parini, p. 78.

CHAPTER 2. PUBLISHED SUCCESS

1. Jackson J. Benson, *The True Adventures of John Steinbeck, Writer* (New York: Penguin Books, 1984), p. 166.

2. Jay Parini, *John Steinbeck, A Biography* (New York: Henry Holt & Company, 1995), pp. 91–92.

3. Ibid., p. 98.

4. Thomas Kiernan, *The Intricate Music: A Biography of John Steinbeck* (Boston: Little Brown and Company, 1970), p. 162.

5. Benson, pp. 219–220.

6. Parini, p. 124.

7. Benson, p. 265.

8. Parini, pp. 105–106.

9. Andre Gide, *The Journals of Andre Gide. Vol. IV, 1939–49* (New York: Alfred A. Knopf, 1951), p. 48.

10. Benson, p. 324.

CHAPTER 3. *OF MICE AND MEN*

1. Herbert N. Foerstel, "Banned in the U.S.A.," n.d., <http://www–2.cs.cmu.edu/People/spok/most-banned.html> (December 13, 2003).

2. Warren French, "End of a Dream," *Steinbeck: A Collection of Critical Essays*, ed. Robert Murray Davis (Englewood Cliffs, N.J.: Prentice–Hall, 1972), p. 64.

3. Ibid., p. 66.

4. Ibid., p. 67.

5. Louis Owens, "Of Mice and Men: The Dream of Commitment," *John Steinbeck*, ed. Harold Bloom (New York: Chelsea House Publishers, 1987), p. 146.

6. Marilyn Chandler McEntyre, "Of Mice and Men: A Story of Innocence Retained," *The Betrayal of Brotherhood in the Work of John Steinbeck: Cain Sign*, ed. Michael J. Meyer (Lewiston: Edwin Mellen Press, 2000), p. 205.

7. French, p. 66.

CHAPTER 4. WRITING THE FIRST "BIG BOOK"

1. Jay Parini, *John Steinbeck, A Biography* (New York: Henry Holt & Company, 1995), pp. 174–177.

2. Charles Wollenberg, "Introduction," *The Harvest Gypsies* (Berkeley: Heydey Books, 1988), xi.

3. Ibid., xiii.

4. Parini, pp. 180–183.

5. Thomas Kiernan, *The Intricate Music: A Biography of John Steinbeck* (Boston: Little Brown and Company, 1970), pp. 217–218.

6. Jackson J. Benson, *The True Adventures of John Steinbeck, Writer* (New York: Penguin Books, 1984), p. 376.

7. Elaine Steinbeck and Robert Wallsten, eds., *Steinbeck: a Life in Letters* (New York: The Viking Press, 1975), p. 159.

8. Parini, p. 199.

9. "The Red Pony," *Ed Stephan's Front Door*, n.d., <http://www.ac.wwu.edu/~stephan/Steinbeck/pony.html> (December 13, 2003).

10. Benson, pp. 391–392.

11. Parini, p. 226.

12. Clifton Fadiman, "Highway 66—A Tale of Five Cities," *The New Yorker*, April 15, 1939, p. 81.

13. Parini, p. 220.

14. Henry R. Luce, ed., *Time Capsule, 1939* (New York: Time, Inc., 1968), p. 211.

CHAPTER 5. *THE GRAPES OF WRATH*

1. Peter Lisca, "The Grapes of Wrath," *Steinbeck: A Collection of Critical Essays*, ed. Robert Murray Davis (Englewood Cliffs, N.J.: Prentice–Hall, 1972), p. 90.

2. Ibid., p. 93.

3. Warren French, "The Social Novel At the End of An Era," n.d., <http://ocean.st.usm.edu/~wsimkins/trans.html> (December 13, 2003).

4. Warren French, *John Steinbeck's Fiction Revisited* (Boston: Twayne Publishers, 1994), p. 81.

5. Lisca, p. 95.

6. Thomas Kiernan, *The Intricate Music: A Biography of John Steinbeck* (Boston: Little Brown and Company, 1970), p. 237.

CHAPTER 6. COPING WITH FAME

1. Jay Parini, *John Steinbeck, A Biography* (New York: Henry Holt & Company, 1995), p. 226.

2. Thomas Kiernan, *The Intricate Music: A Biography of John Steinbeck* (Boston: Little Brown and Company, 1970), p. 243.

3. Ibid., p. 255.

4. Parini, p. 265.

5. Jackson J. Benson, *The True Adventures of John Steinbeck, Writer* (New York: Penguin Books, 1984), p. 542.

6. Parini, p. 305.

7. Kiernan, p. 281.

8. Parini, p. 315.

9. Benson, p. 637.

10. Kiernan, p. 285.

CHAPTER 7. THE LAST BIG BOOK

1. Thomas Kiernan, *The Intricate Music: A Biography of John Steinbeck* (Boston: Little Brown and Company, 1970), p. 285.

2. Jay Parini, *John Steinbeck, A Biography* (New York: Henry Holt & Company, 1995), p. 347.

3. John Steinbeck IV and Nancy Steinbeck, *The Other Side of Eden: Life with John Steinbeck* (New York: Prometheus Books, 2001), p. 80.

4. Pauline Pearson, "East of Eden," *National Steinbeck Center*, June 1995, <http://www.steinbeck.org/EastEden.html> (December 13, 2003).

5. Parini, p. 356.

CHAPTER 8. *EAST OF EDEN*

1. John Steinbeck, *East of Eden* (New York: The Viking Press, 1952), p. 14.

2. Ibid., p. 263.

3. Bruce Ouderkirk, "Fathers and Sons in East of Eden," *Betrayal of Brotherhood in the Work of John Steinbeck,* ed. Michael J. Meyer (Lewiston, Maine: Edwin Mellen Press, 2000), p. 370.

4. Michael J. Meyer, "Endless Possibilities: The Significance of Nomos in Steinbeck's East of Eden," *The Betrayal of Brotherhood in the Work of John Steinbeck: Cain Sign,* ed. Michael J. Meyer (Lewiston: Edwin Mellen Press, 2000), p. 427.

5. Richard F. Peterson, "East of Eden," *A Study Guide to Steinbeck,* ed. Tetsumaro Hayashi (Metuchen, N.J.: Scarecrow Press, 1974), p. 74.

6. John Steinbeck, *East of Eden*, p. 165.

7. John Gribben, "Steinbeck's East of Eden and Milton's Paradise Lost," *Steinbeck Quarterly*, vol.V, no. 2, Spring 1972, p. 40.

8. John Steinbeck, East of Eden, p. 415.

9. Joseph Wood Krutch, "John Steinbeck's Dramatic Tale of Three Generations," *Steinbeck and His Critics, A Record of Twenty-Five Years,* eds. E. W. Tedlock, Jr. and C. V. Wicker (Albuquerque: University of New Mexico Press, 1957), p. 302.

10. Peterson, p. 75.

11. Ibid., p. 76.

12. Ibid., pp. 78–79.

13. John Steinbeck, *East of Eden*, p. 132.

CHAPTER 9. A WRITER WRITES AS HE LIVES

1. "John Steinbeck (1902–1968)," 2003, <http://www.kirjasto.sci.fi/johnstei.htm> (December 13, 2003).

2. Tim Dirks, "East of Eden (1955)," *The Greatest Films*, 1996, <http://www.filmsite.org/east.html> (December 13, 2003).

3. Jay Parini, *John Steinbeck, A Biography* (New York: Henry Holt & Company, 1995), p. 361.

4. Ibid., p. 362.

5. Thomas Kiernan, *The Intricate Music: A Biography of John Steinbeck* (Boston: Little Brown and Company, 1970), p. 310.

6. John Steinbeck IV and Nancy Steinbeck, *The Other Side of Eden: Life with John Steinbeck* (New York: Prometheus Books, 2001), p. 88.

7. Jackson J. Benson, *The True Adventures of John Steinbeck, Writer* (New York: Penguin Books, 1984), p. 754.

8. Parini, p. 376.

9. Ibid., p. 385.

10. Warren French, "The Social Novel At the End of An Era," n.d., <http://ocean.st.usm.edu/~wsimkins/trans.html> (December 13, 2003).

11. Parini, p. 401.

12. Ibid., p. 409.

13. Elia Kazan, *Elia Kazan: A Life* (New York: Doubleday, 1989), p. 786.

14. Parini, p. 420.

15. Ibid., pp. 420–421.

16. John Steinbeck IV and Nancy Steinbeck, pp. 80–81.

17. Parini, p. 434.

CHAPTER 10. THE MEASURE
OF THIS MAN

1. Jay Parini, *John Steinbeck, A Biography* (New York: Henry Holt & Company, 1995), p. 442.

2. Ibid.

3. John Steinbeck IV and Nancy Steinbeck, *The Other Side of Eden: Life with John Steinbeck* (New York: Prometheus Books, 2001), p. 80.

4. Parini, p. 444.

5. Ibid., p. 445.

6. Warren French, "The Social Novel At the End of An Era," n.d., <http://ocean.st.usm.edu/~wsimkins/trans.html> (December 13, 2003).

7. Parini, p. 448.

8. Ibid., p. 449.

9. Ibid., p. 457.

10. Ibid., p. 458.

11. Ibid., p. 471.

12. John Steinbeck IV and Nancy Steinbeck, *The Other Side of Eden: Life with John Steinbeck* (New York: Prometheus Books, 2001), p. 106.

13. Parini, p. 479.

14. Jackson J. Benson, The True Adventures of John Steinbeck, Writer (New York: Penguin Books, 1984), p. 1036.

GLOSSARY

allegory—A symbolic representation or expression.

foreshadow—To hint at something that will happen later in a story.

intercalary—Something inserted between two things or parts.

irony—The use of words to express an idea that is opposite to the words' literal meaning.

metaphor—A figure of speech in which a comparison is made between two words or phrases that have no literal relationship.

personification—A figure of speech in which an inanimate object is treated as, or compared to, a living thing.

phalanx—An organized group of people.

protest novel—A novel with a message about a current social or political condition and calls for change.

symbol—Something that stands for, represents, or suggests another thing.

theme—A distinctive quality or concern in one or more works of fiction.

transcendentalism—The term Transcendentalism comes from the word "transcend," which means "to go beyond." Transcendentalism taught that man was basically good and that human life went beyond the experiences of the physical world.

Selected Published Works of John Steinbeck

Cup of Gold (1929)

The Pastures of Heaven (1932)

To a God Unknown (1933)

Tortilla Flat (1935)

In Dubious Battle (1936)

Of Mice and Men (1937)

The Red Pony (1937)

The Long Valley (1938)

The Grapes of Wrath (1939)

The Forgotten Village (1941)

Sea of Cortez (1941)

The Moon Is Down (1942)

Bombs Away (1942)

The Portable Steinbeck (1943)

Cannery Row (1945)

The Pearl (1947)

The Wayward Bus (1947)

A Russian Journal (1948)

Burning Bright (1950)

The Log from the Sea of Cortez (1951)

East of Eden (1952)

Sweet Thursday (1954)

Pipe Dream (1956)

The Short Reign of Pippin IV (1957)

Once There Was a War (1958)

The Winter of Our Discontent (1961)

Travels with Charley (1962)

America and Americans (1966)

Journal of a Novel (1969)

A Life in Letters (1975)

Viva Zapata! (1975)

Acts of King Arthur and His Noble Nights (1976)

Letters to Elizabeth (1978)

Uncollected Stories of John Steinbeck (1986)

Selected Essays of John Steinbeck (1987)

The Harvest Gypsies (1988)

Working Days (1989)

Movies for Theatrical Showing

Of Mice and Men (1939)

The Grapes of Wrath (1940)

The Forgotten Village (1941)

Tortilla Flat (1942)

The Moon is Down (1943)

Lifeboat (1944)

A Medal for Benny (1945)

The Pearl (1947)

The Red Pony (1949)

Viva Zapata! (1952)

East of Eden (1955)

The Wayward Bus (1957)

Flight (1961)

Cannery Row (1982)

Of Mice and Men (1992)

Movies for Television

Molly Morgan (1950)

O'Henry's Full House (1952)

Nobody's Fool (1954)

Nothing So Monstrous (1954)

The House (1954)

A Medal for Benny (1954)

The Flight (1956)

America and Americans (1967)

Of Mice and Men (1968)

Travels with Charley (1968)

The Harness (1972)

The Red Pony (1973)

FURTHER READING

Bloom, Harold, ed. *John Steinbeck*. Broomall, Pa.: Chelsea House, 1999.

Florence, Donnë. *John Steinbeck: America's Author.* Berkeley Heights, N.J.: Enslow Publishers, Inc., 2000.

Johnson, Claudia Durst. *Understanding* The Grapes of Wrath. Westport, Conn.: Greenwood Press, 1999.

Tessitore, John. *John Steinbeck: A Writer's Life.* Danbury, Conn.: Franklin Watts, Inc., 2001.

Tracy, Kathleen. *John Steinbeck*. Bear, Del.: Mitchell Lane, 2005.

Internet Addresses

National Steinbeck Center
http://www.steinbeck.org/MainFrame.html

The Center for Steinbeck Studies
http://www2.sjsu.edu/steinbeck/

Perspectives in American Literature: John Steinbeck
http://www.csustan.edu/english/reuben/pal/chap7/steinbeck.html

INDEX

A

America and Americans, 151–152
Atlantic Monthly, The, 130 141, 144

B

Ballou, Robert, 25–29
Bear Flag, 126–127
Benet, Stephen Vincent, 91
Biblical Allegory 38, 64–65, 67,
    69–72, 79–80, 85, 86, 105,
    108–113, 117–121
*Bombs Away: The Story of a Bomber
    Team*, 93
Book of the Month Club, The, 52,
    92, 98, 124
Bristol, Horace, 56, 63
Burning Bright, 104

C

Cain and Abel, 38, 105,
    108–113,119–121
Cannery Row, 33, 90, 95–96, 100,
    126, 129
Capa, Robert, 98–99, 128
Chambers, Pat, 30
Colliers Magazine, 106
Collins, Tom, 50–51, 52–54, 56, 82
Commonwealth Magazine, 98
Conger,Gwyn, 89–99, 102, 113,
    127, 141, 150
Courier-Journal, 132, 137
Cousins, Norman, 129
Covici, Pascal "Pat," 30, 31, 57–60,
    106, 134, 136, 141, 151
Covici-Friede, 30, 31, 56
Cox, Denton, 157
Cup of Gold, 17, 19–22

D

Dean, James, 124
Decker, Bill, 18
Decker, Caroline, 30

Don Keehan, 134–135
Don Quixote, 134

E

East of Eden, 5, 38, 104–106, 108–125
Eisenhower, Dwight, 125–126, 131
Emerson, Ralph Waldo, 64, 70
Esquire, 133, 137

F

Fadiman, Clifton, 62, 92
Fonda, Henry, 134–135
Foreign Information Service, 91, 93
Forgotten Village, The, 66, 90, 96

G

Gide, Andre, 32
"Gifts of Iban, The," 17
Grapes of Gladness, 63
Grapes of Wrath, The, 33, 38, 57–63,
    64–87, 88–89, 92, 94, 96, 106,
    133, 135, 141, 146, 153
Great Depression, The, 19, 22, 25,
    36
Guggenheim, Harry A., 152, 154
Guinzburg, Alice, 145
Guinzburg, Harold, 143, 145
Guinzburg, Tom, 151

H

Hammerstein, Oscar, 11, 127–130
Harvest Gypsies, The, 52
Hellman, Lillian, 107
Hemingway, Ernest, 19, 65
Henning, Carol, 18, 19, 21–26, 28,
    29, 33–34, 53, 54, 57–59, 89–92
Hitchcock, Alfred, 93–94
Holiday magazine, 132, 137, 141
Holt, Guy, 16, 17
"How Mr. Hogan Robbed a Bank,"
    130
HUAC, 106–107, 125, 133–134

I

In Dubious Battle, 30–33, 106

J

Johnson, Lyndon B., 126, 149, 153–155
Journal of a Novel: The "East of Eden" Letters, 105

K

Kaufman, George, 8, 53
Kazan, Elia, 102, 104, 106–107, 124–125, 137
Kazin, Alfred, 134–135, 147
Kennedy, Jacqueline, 126
Kennedy, John F., 126, 140, 148–149
King Arthur 31, 35, 136, 152
Knights of the Round Table, 132–134, 136

L

"Lady in Infra-Red, A," 14, 17
L'Affaire Lettuceberg, 55
"Letters to Alicia," 152
Life Magazine, 56, 63, 141
Lifeboat, 93–94
Log of the Sea of Cortez, The, 90, 104
Long Valley, The, 58

M

Malory, Sir Thomas, 7, 132–134, 136, 137, 152
McCarthy, Mary, 32
McNally, Terrence, 142–143, 148, 150
Medal for Benny, A, 93
Migrant workers, 36, 48–52, 55–57, 63, 65, 80–81
Milestone, Lewis, 90, 95
Miller, Ted, 16, 18, 24
Mirrielees, Edith Ronald, 11, 13, 15
Mizener, Arthur, 146–147
Moby Dick, 37
Moon Is Down, The, 91–93, 97
Morte D'Arthur, 7, 132–133

N

Nation, 32, 52, 125
National Labor Relations Act, 56
National Review, The, 62
New York American, 15
New York Board of Censors, 90
New York Drama Critics Circle, The, 54
New York Herald Tribune, 94, 98
New York Times, The, 92, 125, 134, 144, 145
New Yorker, The, 62
Newsday, 152, 154–155
Newsweek, 144, 155
Nobel Prize, 144–147
North American Review, 28

O

O'Hara, John, 99, 148
Of Mice and Men, 13, 34, 35–47, 48, 52–55, 57, 88, 90, 91
Okies, 29, 48–50, 63, 79–81, 88
"Old Curmudgeon, The," 137–138
Once There Was a War, 95
Other Side of Eden, The, 127
Otis, Elizabeth, 28, 30, 31, 34, 55, 56, 60, 129, 136–139, 157
Our Town, 54

P

Paradise Lost, 33, 118
Pastures of Heaven, The, 24, 25, 30
"People to People," 132
People, Yes, The, 65
Pearl, The, 95–97, 99
Peterson, Richard E., 151–152
Phalanx theory, 27, 33, 47, 55, 71, 75, 82, 83, 93, 122–123
Pipe Dream, 127, 129
Presidential Medal of Freedom, 150–151
Protest Novel, 64–65
Pulitzer Prize, 89

R

Red Pony, The, 28, 59, 90, 100

Ricketts, Edward F., 23–25, 27, 33, 34, 75, 89–90, 96, 100–101, 107, 128–129
Roosevelt Administration, 51, 91
Roosevelt, Eleanor, 88, 90
Russian Journal, The, 99

S

Salinas, 6, 7, 8, 10, 13, 26, 45, 51, 59, 158
Salinas High School 7, 8
Salinas Valley, 104
San Francisco News, 48–52, 82
Sandburg, Carl, 65, 138
Saturday Review, 129, 132, 137
Scott, Elaine, 103–105, 126–132, 135–145, 148–150, 154–158
Scott, Waverly, 104, 127, 131
Sheffield, Carlton "Dook," 11, 13, 14, 20–22, 95
Short Reign of Pippin IV, The, 130, 133
Smith, Elizabeth, a.k.a. John Breck ,14, 15
Smoker's Companion, The, 17
"Something That Happened," 33–34
Soviet Union ,53, 98–99, 133–134, 148–149
Stanford University, 8, 9, 11, 15, 17, 137
Starvation Under the Orange Trees, 52
Steinbeck, Beth, 6,7, 15, 25, 140
Steinbeck, Esther ,6, 140
Steinbeck, John, 11, 6, 19, 21, 24–26, 31
Steinbeck, John IV 97, 102–105, 108, 120–121, 126–128, 131, 141–144, 149–150, 153–157
Steinbeck, Mary, 6, 7, 18, 19, 132, 151
Steinbeck, Nancy, 126, 141

Steinbeck, Olive, 6, 7, 24–27, 29, 108
Steinbeck, Thom, 95, 102–105, 108, 120–121, 126–128, 131, 141–144, 149–150, 157
Stevenson, Adlai ,125, 131, 138
Sweet Thursday, 33, 126–130

T

Thoreau, Henry David, 70, 144
Time Magazine, 62
Timshel, 105, 113, 116–118
"To a Mouse," 34
To an Unknown God, 22, 25, 28
Tortilla Flat, 28-32, 128
Travels with a Donkey, 139–140
Travels with Charley, 139–141, 143, 144, 151
Truth About John Steinbeck and the Migrants, The, 63

U

Uncle Tom's Cabin, 62

V

Valenti, Jack, 153
Van Doren, Mark ,103
Vietnam, 128, 153–156
Viva Zapata, 102–104, 124

W

War and Peace, 65
Wayward Bus, The, 97–98
Weedpatch, 50–51, 56, 81–83
Whitman, Walt, 64, 65, 70
Wilder, Thornton, 54, 91
Winter of Our Discontent, The, 130–131, 137–139, 141, 148
World War I, 8
World War II, 91–95, 131, 132, 154

Z

Zanuck, Darryl, 63
Zapata, Emiliano, 96